I'm convinced that the Bible is somehow powerfully sin[ ]
complex. Like a diamond viewed from different angles, [   ]
confronts my heart in fresh ways. This Bible-study series offers insightful
perspectives and gives its participants a refreshing opportunity to admire the
character of God and be transformed by the truth of his Word. Our souls need
to meander through the minutiae and metanarrative of the Bible, and the
Storyline Bible Studies help us do both.

> KYLE IDLEMAN, senior pastor of Southeast Christian Church and bestselling author of *Not a Fan*
> and *One at a Time*

If you are longing for a breath of fresh air in your spiritual life, this study is
for you. Kat Armstrong brings to life both familiar and less familiar Bible
stories in such an engaging way that you can't help but see how the God of
the past is also working and moving in your present. Through the captivating
truths revealed in this series, you will discover more about God's faithfulness,
be equipped to move past fear and disappointment, and be empowered to be
who you were created to be. If your faith has felt mundane or routine, these
words will be a refreshing balm to your soul and a guide to go deeper in your
relationship with God.

> HOSANNA WONG, international speaker and bestselling author of *How (Not) to Save the World:
> The Truth about Revealing God's Love to the People Right Next to You*

We are watching a new wave of Bible studies that care about the Bible's big
story, from Genesis to Revelation; that plunge Bible readers into the depths
of human despair and show them the glories of the Kingdom God plans
for creation; and that invite readers to participate in that story in all its
dimensions—in the mountains and the valleys. Anyone who ponders these
Bible studies will come to terms not only with the storyline of the Bible but
also with where each of us fits in God's grand narrative. I heartily commend
Kat's **Storyline Bible Studies**.

> REV. CANON DR. SCOT MCKNIGHT, professor of New Testament at Northern Seminary

Kat Armstrong is an able trail guide with contagious enthusiasm! In this series, she'll take you hiking through Scripture to experience mountains and valleys, sticks and stones, sinners and saints. If you are relatively new to the Bible or are struggling to see how it all fits together, your trek with Kat will be well worth it. You might even decide that hiking through the Bible is your new hobby.

CARMEN JOY IMES, associate professor of Old Testament at Biola University and author of *Bearing God's Name: Why Sinai Still Matters*

Kat Armstrong takes you into the heart of Scripture so that Scripture can grow in your heart. The **Storyline Bible Studies** have everything: the overarching story of God's redemption, the individual biblical story's historical context, and the text's interpretation that connects with today's realities. Armstrong asks insightful questions that make the Bible come alive and draws authentically on her own faith journey so that readers might deepen their relationship with Jesus. Beautifully written and accessible, the **Storyline Bible Studies** are a wonderful resource for individual or group study.

LYNN H. COHICK, PHD, provost and dean of academic affairs at Northern Seminary

Christians affirm that the Bible is God's Word and provides God's life-giving instruction and encouragement. But what good is such an authoritative and valuable text if God's people don't engage it to find the help the Scriptures provide? Here's where Kat Armstrong's studies shine. In each volume, she presents Bible study as a journey through Scripture that can be transformational. In the process, she enables readers to see the overarching storyline of the Bible and to find their place in that story. In addition, Armstrong reinforces the essential steps that make Bible study life-giving for people seeking to grow in their faith. Whether for individuals, for small groups, or as part of a church curriculum, these studies are ideally suited to draw students into a fresh and invigorating engagement with God's Word.

WILLIAM W. KLEIN, PHD, professor emeritus of New Testament interpretation and author of *Handbook for Personal Bible Study: Enriching Your Experience with God's Word*

Kat has done two things that I love. She's taken something that is familiar and presented it in a fresh way that is understandable by all, balancing the profound with accessibility. And her trustworthy and constant approach to Bible study equips the participant to emerge from this study with the ability to keep studying and growing more.

MARTY SOLOMON, creator and executive producer of *The BEMA Podcast*

You are in for an adventure. In this series, Kat pulls back the curtain to reveal how intentionally God has woven together seemingly disconnected moments in the collective Bible story. Her delivery is both brilliant and approachable. She will invite you to be a curious sleuth as you navigate familiar passages of Scripture, discovering things you'd never seen before. I promise you will never read the living Word the same again.

JENN JETT BARRETT, founder and visionary of The Well Summit

Kat has done it again! The same wisdom, depth, humility, and authenticity that we have come to expect from her previous work is on full display here in her new **Storyline Bible Study** series. Kat is the perfect guide through these important themes and through the story of Scripture: gentle and generous on the one hand, capable and clear on the other. She is a gifted communicator and teacher of God's Word. The format of these studies is helpful too— perfect pacing, just the right amount of new information at each turn, with plenty of space for writing and prayerful reflection as you go and some great resources for further study. I love learning from Kat, and I'm sure you will too. Grab a few friends from your church or neighborhood and dig into these incredible resources together to find your imagination awakened and your faith strengthened.

DAN LOWERY, president of Pillar Seminary

Kat Armstrong possesses something I deeply admire: a sincere and abiding respect for the Bible. Her tenaciousness to know more about her beloved Christ, her commitment to truth telling, and her desire to dig until she mines the deepest gold for her Bible-study readers makes her one of my favorite Bible teachers. I find few that match her scriptural attentiveness and even fewer that embody her humble spirit. This project is stunning, like the rest of her work.

LISA WHITTLE, bestselling author of *Jesus over Everything: Uncomplicating the Daily Struggle to Put Jesus First*, Bible teacher, and podcast host

SAINTS

ENJOYING A RELATIONSHIP WITH JESUS
WHEN YOU'RE DISILLUSIONED WITH RELIGION

KAT ARMSTRONG

A NavPress resource published in alliance
with Tyndale House Publishers

NavPress is the publishing ministry of The Navigators, an international Christian organization and leader in personal spiritual development. NavPress is committed to helping people grow spiritually and enjoy lives of meaning and hope through personal and group resources that are biblically rooted, culturally relevant, and highly practical.

For more information, visit NavPress.com.

Saints: Enjoying a Relationship with Jesus When You're Disillusioned with Religion

Copyright © 2023 by Kat Armstrong. All rights reserved.

A NavPress resource published in alliance with Tyndale House Publishers

NavPress and the NavPress logo are registered trademarks of NavPress, The Navigators, Colorado Springs, CO. *Tyndale* is a registered trademark of Tyndale House Ministries. Absence of ® in connection with marks of NavPress or other parties does not indicate an absence of registration of those marks.

The Team:
David Zimmerman, Publisher; Caitlyn Carlson, Acquisitions Editor; Elizabeth Schroll, Copy Editor; Olivia Eldredge, Operations Manager; Julie Chen, Designer; Sarah K. Johnson and Ian K. Smith, Proofreaders

Cover illustration by Lindsey Bergsma. Copyright © 2023 by NavPress/The Navigators. All rights reserved.

Author photo by Judy Rodriguez, copyright © 2021. All rights reserved.

Author is represented by Jana Burson of The Christopher Ferebee Agency, christopherferebee.com

Some of the anecdotal illustrations in this book are true to life and are included with the permission of the persons involved. All other illustrations are composites of real situations, and any resemblance to people living or dead is purely coincidental.

For information about special discounts for bulk purchases, please contact Tyndale House Publishers at csresponse@tyndale.com, or call 1-855-277-9400.

ISBN 978-1-64158-600-9

Printed in the United States of America

29	28	27	26	25	24	23
7	6	5	4	3	2	1

For my dad, Ronald K. Obenhaus.
I think you would have loved this.

Contents

A Message from Kat

"MY CONFIDENCE in Christian leaders is at an all-time low."

My friend had called me to process the disillusionment that naturally follows seeing Christian leaders fall. And her words resonated with me. We are in a season filled with headlines that confirm the profound brokenness of celebrity Christianity, a system that dehumanizes the celebrity and traumatizes their followers.

My friend articulated something that stunned me: She braces herself every Sunday night to see which Christian pastor or leader used their Sunday service to announce their failure of character. As she internalizes the foreboding dread of Sunday nights, she's shaken in her soul.

When fellow followers of Jesus—and leaders we look up to—continue to disappoint us, reconciling the failures of humans with an unshakable faith in Christ might be the single most important endeavor you and I need to pursue. That's why we go to God's Word: to center our faith on Jesus. Not on our favorite preacher, the bestselling author that changed our life, or the Christians annoying us on social media. Our hope is in Jesus. He is the pioneer and perfecter of our faith (Hebrews 12:2). He's our foundational truth.

Jesus never fails. And he won't fail you.

My friend said something in our conversation I'll never forget: All the moral failures of her spiritual heroes and all the reckoning within the church isn't just undermining her trust in leaders and herself—it's causing her to question whether Christianity itself is valid. If God's people are not Christlike, and becoming like Christ is the point of Christianity, is the way of Christ true?

If you're asking this question as well, let me hold this space for you. But let me also say to you: The way of Christ cannot be undone or shaken by the failures of his people. Not by our leaders, not by our friends, not even by ourselves.

God never tried to hide the reality of fallen humanity in the pages of inspired Scripture. One of the ways he made sure we can anchor our faith in Jesus was by telling the truth in the Bible about how even the seemingly best of us can get it wrong. God could have easily omitted these stories, but instead, he chose to magnify these failures in unflattering characterizations—archetypes that represent religious authorities falling short. He did so to prove we *all* need a Savior.

And he *is* the Savior.

My own concerns about the credibility of Christian leaders sent me into the Scriptures to study New Testament characters—messed-up religious people acting foolishly. In some providential way, uncovering this archetype in God's Word filled me with hope and peace. Hope that God continues to hold people accountable, uses broken people, and restores us when we repent. And peace—that I can still enjoy a relationship with Jesus when religious leaders fall and religion feels unstable.

Whether you are new to the Christian faith or a seasoned Bible reader, I'm praying that your time studying saintly characters in the Bible is an awe-inspiring catalyst to engage and experience God's truth—that you would marvel at the artistry of God's storytelling. And that you would see, as you sit in the stories of these broken leaders, that not even the most painful human failures can disrupt God's work and his deep love for you.

Love,

Kat

The Storyline of Scripture

YOUR DECISION TO STUDY THE BIBLE for the next few weeks is no accident—God has brought you here, to this moment. And I don't want to take it for granted. Here, at the beginning, I want to invite you into the most important step you can take, the one that brings the whole of the Bible alive in extraordinary ways: a relationship with Jesus.

The Bible is a collection of divinely inspired manuscripts written over fifteen hundred years by at least forty different authors. Together, the manuscripts make up tens of thousands of verses, sixty-six books, and two testaments. Point being: It's a lot of content.

But the Bible is really just one big story: God's story of redemption. From Genesis to Revelation the Bible includes narratives, songs, poems, wisdom literature, letters, and even apocalyptic prophecies. Yet everything we read in God's Word helps us understand God's love and his plan to be in a relationship with us.

If you hear nothing else, hear this: God loves you.

It's easy to get lost in the vast amount of information in the Bible, so we're going to explore the storyline of Scripture in four parts. And as you locate your experience in the story of the Bible, I hope the story of redemption becomes your own.

PART 1: GOD MADE SOMETHING GOOD.

The big story—God's story of redemption—started in a garden. When God launched his project for humanity, he purposed all of us—his image bearers—to flourish and co-create with him. In the beginning there was peace, beauty, order, and abundant life. The soil was good. Life was good. We rarely hear this part of our story, but it doesn't make it less true. God created something good—and that includes you.

PART 2: WE MESSED IT UP.

If you've ever thought, *This isn't how it's supposed to be*, you're right. It's not. We messed up God's good world. Do you ever feel like you've won gold medals in messing things up? Me too. All humanity shares in that brokenness. We are imperfect. The people we love are imperfect. Our systems are jacked, and our world is broken. And that's on us. We made the mess, and we literally can't help ourselves. We need to be rescued from our circumstances, the systems in which we live, and ourselves.

PART 3: JESUS MAKES IT RIGHT.

The good news is that God can clean up all our messes, and he does so through the life, death, and resurrection of Jesus Christ. No one denies that Jesus lived and died. That's just history. It's the empty tomb and the hundreds of eyewitnesses who saw Jesus after his death that make us scratch our heads. Because science can only prove something that is repeatable, we are dependent upon the eyewitness testimonies of Jesus' resurrection for this once-in-history moment. If Jesus rose from the dead—and I believe he did—Jesus is exactly who he said he was, and he accomplished exactly what had been predicted for thousands of years. He restored us. Jesus made *it*, all of it, right. He can forgive your sins and connect you to the holy God through his life, death, and resurrection.

PART 4: ONE DAY, GOD WILL MAKE ALL THINGS NEW.

The best news is that this is not as good as it gets. A day is coming when Christ will return. He's coming back to re-create our world: a place with no tears, no pain, no suffering, no brokenness, no helplessness—just love. God will make all things new. In the meantime, God invites you to step into his storyline, to join him in his work of restoring all things. Rescued restorers live with purpose and on mission: not a life devoid of hardship, but one filled with enduring hope.

RESPONDING TO GOD'S STORYLINE

If the storyline of Scripture feels like a lightbulb turning on in your soul, that, my friend, is the one true, living God, who eternally exists as Father, Son, and Holy Spirit. God is inviting you into a relationship with him to have your sins forgiven and secure a place in his presence forever. When you locate your story within God's story of redemption, you begin a lifelong relationship with God that brings meaning, hope, and restoration to your life.

Take a moment now to begin a relationship with Christ:

God, I believe the story of the Bible, that Jesus is Lord and you raised him from the dead to forgive my sins and make our relationship possible. Your storyline is now my story. I want to learn how to love you and share your love with others. Amen.

If you confess with your lips that Jesus is Lord and believe in your heart that God raised him from the dead, you will be saved.

ROMANS 10:9, NRSV

How to Use This Bible Study

THE **STORYLINE BIBLE STUDIES** are versatile and can be used for

+ individual study (self-paced),
+ small groups (five- or ten-lesson curriculum), or
+ church ministry (semester-long curriculum).

INDIVIDUAL STUDY

Each lesson in the *Saints* Bible study is divided into four fifteen- to twenty-minute parts (sixty to eighty minutes of individual study time per lesson). You can work through the material one part at a time over a few different days or all in one sitting. Either way, this study will be like anything good in your life: What you put in, you get out. Each of the four parts of each lesson will help you practice Bible-study methods.

SMALL GROUPS

Working through the *Saints* Bible study with a group could be a catalyst for life change. Although the Holy Spirit can teach you truth when you read the Bible on your own, I want to encourage you to gather a small group together to work through this study for these reasons:

+ God himself is in communion as one essence and three persons: Father, Son, and Holy Spirit.
+ Interconnected, interdependent relationships are hallmarks of the Christian faith life.
+ When we collaborate with each other in Bible study, we have access to the viewpoints of our brothers and sisters in Christ, which enrich our understanding of the truth.

For this Bible study, every small-group member will need a copy of the *Saints* study guide. In addition, I've created a free downloadable small-group guide that includes

+ discussion questions for each lesson,
+ Scripture readings, and
+ prayer prompts.

Whether you've been a discussion leader for decades or just volunteered to lead a group for the first time, you'll find the resources you need to create a loving atmosphere for men and women to grow in Christlikeness. You can download the small-group guide using this QR code.

CHURCH MINISTRY

Church and ministry leaders: Your work is sacred. I know that planning and leading through a semester of ministry can be both challenging and rewarding. That's why every **Storyline Bible Study** is written so that you can build modular semesters of ministry. The *Saints* Bible study is designed to complement the

Sinners Bible study. Together, *Sinners* and *Saints* can support a whole semester of ministry seamlessly, inviting the people you lead into God's Word and making your life simpler.

To further equip church and ministry leaders, I've created *The Leader's Guide*, a free digital resource. You can download *The Leader's Guide* using this QR code.

The Leader's Guide offers these resources:

+ a sample ministry calendar for a ten-plus-lesson semester of ministry,
+ small-group discussion questions for each lesson,
+ Scripture readings for each lesson,
+ prayer prompts for each lesson,
+ five teaching topics for messages that could be taught in large-group settings, and
+ resources for deeper study.

SPECIAL FEATURES

However you decide to utilize the *Saints* Bible study, whether for individual, self-paced devotional time; as a small-group curriculum; or for semester-long church ministry, you'll notice several stand-out features unique to the **Storyline Bible Studies**:

+ gospel presentation at the beginning of each Bible study;
+ full Scripture passages included in the study so that you can mark up the text and keep your notes in one place;
+ insights from diverse scholars, authors, and Bible teachers;
+ an emphasis on close readings of large portions of Scripture;
+ following one theme instead of focusing on one verse or passage;
+ Christological narrative theology without a lot of church-y words; and
+ retrospective or imaginative readings of the Bible to help Christians follow the storyline of Scripture.

You may have studied the Bible by book, topic, or passage before; all those approaches are enriching ways to read the Word of God. The **Storyline Bible Studies** follow a literary thread to deepen your appreciation for God's master plan of redemption and develop your skill in connecting the Old Testament to the New.

THE SAINTS STORYLINE

EVERY PERSON WE SURVEY in this Bible study is deeply embedded in an ancient, symbol-driven world where the characters of a story don't just exist—they also represent concepts larger than the people themselves. Sometimes God repurposes character archetypes to emphasize particular themes. The theme we'll be exploring in this study is a cautionary tale for Christians and Christian leaders—none of us are above the actions described in the Bible. And yet God moves and works and draws us to himself, even as those created in his image fail.

The *Saints* Bible study will guide you through five Bible stories in which a person acts unrighteously even though they are committed to God. Their presence in the Scriptures is a key element in the story, embodying truths about God's holiness and grace.

I want to address a potential pitfall of studying a type of person in the Scriptures and connecting foil characters in one Bible study: We're going to be tempted to reduce people to their worst mistakes—to write off types of people. You might read about disloyal disciples, power-hungry high priests, and confused Pharisees only to grow cynical and suspicious of everyone who shared the same title: disciple, high priest, or Pharisee. But I hope you dig deeper and see the bigger picture.

Beyond these disappointing characters is a God whose loyal love never fails, who is always entrusting others with his power, and who always brings clarity to our lives. Unrighteous "saints" are not a new problem, and we don't need a new solution. Furthermore, the point of this study is not to identify a character type and then vilify them or generalize their failures in a way that implicates every person like them. The point is to identify *with* their failures and see that all of us are still offered a deep relationship with Jesus based on his grace.

In *Saints*, we're going to explore

+ *John 3, 7, 19*: Nicodemus, the Pharisee disoriented by Jesus' testimony;
+ *John 6, 12, 13, 18*: Judas, the disciple who sold Jesus out;
+ *John 11, 18; Acts 4*: Caiaphas, the high priest unwilling to steward his power generously;
+ *John 18, 21*: Peter, the disciple who denied being connected to Jesus; and
+ *Acts 8; 1 Timothy 1*: Paul, the Pharisee who persecuted Christians.

We're going to do this by looking at each person through four different lenses:

+ **PART 1: CONTEXT.** Do you ever feel dropped into a Bible story disoriented? Part 1 will introduce you to the character you're going to study and help you study their story in its scriptural context. Getting your bearings before you read will enable you to answer the question *What am I about to read?*

+ **PART 2: SEEING.** Do you ever read on autopilot? I do too. Sometimes I finish reading without a clue as to what just happened. A better way to read the Bible is to practice thoughtful, close reading of Scripture to absorb the message God is offering to us. That's why part 2 includes close Scripture reading and observation questions to empower you to answer the question *What is the story saying?*

+ **PART 3: UNDERSTANDING.** If you've ever scratched your head after reading your Bible, part 3 will give you the tools to understand the author's intended meaning both for the original audience and for you. Plus you'll practice connecting the Old and New Testaments to get a fuller picture of God's unchanging grace. Part 3 will enable you to answer the question *What does it mean?*

+ **PART 4: RESPONDING.** The purpose of Bible study is to help you become more Christlike; that's why part 4 will include journaling space for your reflection on and responses to the content and a blank checklist for actionable next steps. You'll be able to process what you're learning so that you can live out the concepts and pursue Christlikeness. Part 4 will enable you to answer the questions *What truths is this passage teaching?* and *How do I apply this to my life?*

One of my prayers for you, as a curious Bible reader, is that our journey through this study will help you cultivate a biblical imagination so that you're able to make connections throughout the whole storyline of the Bible. In each lesson, I'll do my best to include a few verses from different places in the Bible that are connected to our characters. In the course of this study, we'll see the way God shows up for people throughout his Word—and get a glimpse of how he might show up in our lives today.

God's Word is so wonderful, I hardly know how to contain my excitement. Feel free to geek out with me; let your geek flag fly high, my friends. When we can see how interrelated all the parts of Scripture are to each other, we'll find our affection for God stirred as we see his artistic brilliance unfold.

ACCEPTING JESUS' WORDS WHEN THEY CHALLENGE YOUR WORLDVIEW

**NICODEMUS:
THE PHARISEE WHO IS DISORIENTED BY JESUS' TESTIMONY**

SCRIPTURE: JOHN 3, 7, 19

PART 1

CONTEXT

Before you begin your study, we will start with the context of the story we are about to read together: the setting, both cultural and historical; the people involved; and where our passage fits in the larger setting of Scripture. All these things help us make sense of what we're reading. Understanding the context of a Bible story is fundamental to reading Scripture well. Getting your bearings before you read will enable you to answer the question *What am I about to read?*

YEARS AGO, the TV series *Lost* sucked me in. I had to see the show all the way through even though I *lost* interest long before the show ended—I needed to justify the significant investment of time I'd put into the early seasons. Also, I was determined to find answers to all my lingering questions. Surely, I thought, the creators of *Lost* would finally bring clarity to my confusion.

Part of the plot was introducing new people as "the others." The new characters, "the others," had a dual purpose. They helped the writers of the show start a new plotline while at the same time making a broader statement about humanity: We tend to reject people we don't understand.

I bring up "the others" from *Lost* because I want to hedge off any assumptions you and I might make about Nicodemus, the Pharisee we are about to study. It's possible we might come to the Bible assuming that the Pharisees = all Jews = all legalistic.

Although the New Testament writers present some Pharisees as foils or as archetypes of religious people, missing Jesus as the Messiah, we also have examples like Nicodemus and Paul: Pharisees who at first resisted Jesus as the Messiah but then end up changing their minds about Christ. Just because some of the Pharisees misjudged Jesus or struggled to reconcile their interpretation of the law with his claim to fulfill it doesn't make all Pharisees the epitome of legalism or enemies of the Christian faith. Two things can be true at the same time. Some Pharisees in the Bible missed Jesus as the Messiah, and also, not all Pharisees were "bad."

Pharisees like Nicodemus can be reminders that accepting Jesus' words—especially when his truth challenges our worldview—is hard. Sometimes religious people, the ones who are assumed to be the most likely to "get it" . . . don't.

Or, if I may be so bold as to rephrase my point: Sometimes *we* don't get it.

The Pharisees serve as a literary archetype in the Bible's narrative. They are the well-intentioned group of God's people trying to find a way to live up to the law's standards while also accepting their humanness. When Jesus appeared as the fulfillment of their way of life, some of the Pharisees missed it, including Nicodemus.

What you are about to read is a story about a man who was curious enough to approach Jesus with his questions but confused enough to reject his answers. Nicodemus eventually came around to faith in Christ. But Nicodemus's example

In popular Jewish imagination, the Pharisees are the respected teachers of Second Temple Judaism: the ones who extended the holiness of the temple beyond the priests to the people; the ones who insisted on free will along with divine care; the ones who, because of their openness to innovation and concern for the Jewish people as a whole, helped the tradition survive the destruction of the temple in 70 CE.[1]

Joseph Sievers and Amy-Jill Levine, *The Pharisees*

shows us we are not the only people who have ever tried to reconcile Jesus' truth with our human traditions. We are not the only people who seek Jesus in the dark nights of the soul. And we are not alone in our struggle to accept Jesus' testimony of truth as superior to our past views.

If you are trying to put your faith back together and wrestling with the claims of Christ, you're in good company. Nicodemus will show us that sometimes we just need more time with Jesus to fully understand the truth.

So take your time in this lesson. God will not rush you. He is patient.

If God treats us anything like he did Nicodemus, he will welcome your questions, offer you answers, embody his claims, and prove he is trustworthy.

1. **PERSONAL CONTEXT: What is going on in your life right now that might impact how you understand this Bible character?**

2. **SPIRITUAL CONTEXT: If you've never studied this Bible character before, what piques your curiosity? If you've studied this character before, what impressions and insights do you recall?**

SEEING

Seeing the text is vital if we want the heart of the Scripture passage to sink in. We read slowly and intentionally through the text with the context in mind. As we practice close, thoughtful reading of Scripture, we pick up on phrases, implications, and meanings we might otherwise have missed. Part 2 includes close Scripture reading and observation questions to empower you to answer the question *What is the story saying?*

1. **Read John 3:1-21 and circle everything Nicodemus says to Jesus.**

3 There was a man from the Pharisees named Nicodemus, a ruler of the Jews. ² This man came to him at night and said, "Rabbi, we know that you are a teacher who has come from God, for no one could perform these signs you do unless God were with him."

³ Jesus replied, "Truly I tell you, unless someone is born again, he cannot see the kingdom of God."

⁴ "How can anyone be born when he is old?" Nicodemus asked him. "Can he enter his mother's womb a second time and be born?"

⁵ Jesus answered, "Truly I tell you, unless someone is born of water and the Spirit, he cannot enter the kingdom of God. ⁶ Whatever is born of the flesh is flesh, and whatever is born of the Spirit is spirit. ⁷ Do not

be amazed that I told you that you must be born again. [8] The wind blows where it pleases, and you hear its sound, but you don't know where it comes from or where it is going. So it is with everyone born of the Spirit."

[9] "How can these things be?" asked Nicodemus.

[10] "Are you a teacher of Israel and don't know these things?" Jesus replied. [11] "Truly I tell you, we speak what we know and we testify to what we have seen, but you do not accept our testimony. [12] If I have told you about earthly things and you don't believe, how will you believe if I tell you about heavenly things? [13] No one has ascended into heaven except the one who descended from heaven—the Son of Man.

[14] "Just as Moses lifted up the snake in the wilderness, so the Son of Man must be lifted up, [15] so that everyone who believes in him may have eternal life. [16] For God loved the world in this way: He gave his one and only Son, so that everyone who believes in him will not perish but have eternal life. [17] For God did not send his Son into the world to condemn the world, but to save the world through him. [18] Anyone who believes in him is not condemned, but anyone who does not believe is already condemned, because he has not believed in the name of the one and only Son of God. [19] This is the judgment: The light has come into the world, and people loved darkness rather than the light because their deeds were evil. [20] For everyone who does evil hates the light and avoids it, so that his deeds may not be exposed. [21] But anyone who lives by the truth comes to the light, so that his works may be shown to be accomplished by God."

JOHN 3:1-21

John 3:1 identifies Nicodemus as a Pharisee, or a ruler of the people. Since so much time and history stand between us and the Pharisees, here are some facts about the Pharisees:

+ All Pharisees were Jewish, but not all Jews were Pharisees.

+ The Pharisees were a group of devout, God-fearing Jews who represented a school of thought known for interpreting the law—the law given by God to the Israelites at Mount Sinai—precisely. But not so they could exclude or condemn. Quite the opposite. They were known for their leniency.[2]

+ Pharisees were known for applying the law in a way that created less severe punishment for sins. For instance, they resisted capital punishment. Compared to the priests, they were lenient with the law.

+ Pharisees believed that a Messiah was coming and that resurrection from the dead was the future of righteous people.

2. **Reflecting on what we just learned about Pharisees, why do you think Nicodemus came to Jesus? What could his motivation have been for approaching Jesus with his questions? List anything that comes to mind.**

The Pharisees were less the conservative preservers of the status quo and more countercultural teachers and creative innovators who offered popular, lenient alternative teachings to the stringency promoted by the priests in the temple and the covenanters at Qumran.[3]

Joseph Sievers and Amy-Jill Levine, *The Pharisees*

3. What did Nicodemus know about Jesus before this conversation? (See John 3:1-2.)

4. What did Jesus tell Nicodemus was required to see the Kingdom of God? (See John 3:3.)

Nicodemus responded to Jesus by asking how these things could be true. I love Nicodemus. I'd want to know the same thing had I been in this conversation with Jesus. I would have said, "But how, though?"

5. What faith questions would you bring up to Jesus if he were standing right in front of you?

6. In your own words, paraphrase what Jesus says to Nicodemus in John 3:16-17.

If Nicodemus, like all Pharisees, believed a Messiah was coming, Jesus' claims to be the Son of God and the Savior of the world would have required investigation.

Nicodemus couldn't accept Jesus' words in the moment, but he also couldn't ignore his desire to learn more—because he believed that the law didn't judge a person until their testimony was heard and their actions could be proved.

Notice, for example, how Nicodemus responded to a crowd who wanted to condemn Jesus in John 7:50-51: "Nicodemus—the one who came to him previously and who was one of them—said to them, 'Our law doesn't judge a man before it hears from him and knows what he's doing, does it?'"

7. When Jesus used the metaphor of light in this conversation, he was referring to himself. Jesus is the Light of the World. Replace every instance of *light* or *the light* in John 3:19-21 by filling in each blank with the name *Jesus*:

¹⁹ "This is the judgment: _____ has come into the world, and people loved darkness rather than _____ because their deeds were evil. ²⁰ For everyone who does evil hates _____ and avoids _____, so that his deeds may not be exposed. ²¹ But anyone who lives by the truth comes to _____, so that his works may be shown to be accomplished by God."

JOHN 3:19-21

8. **How do you imagine Nicodemus responded to this conversation? Check any options that seem possible. Next to your choice(s), write out a phrase that explains why you might have expected this reaction.**

☐ confused

☐ speechless

☐ frustrated

☐ hopeful

☐ curious

☐ intrigued

☐ intent

☐ doubtful

☐ amazed

☐ shocked

☐ resistant

☐ other:

In view of the obviously symbolic function of "night" in the Gospel, and the scriptural association of darkness with ignorance or lack of understanding, this visit at night may illustrate what will be spelled out later in the chapter: "the light has come into the world" (3:19) to bring people out of darkness.[4]

Marianne Meye Thompson, *John: A Commentary*

Before we move on to a deeper understanding of the meaning of this conversation, I want to point out that Nicodemus came to Jesus in the dark. Many scholars speculate why he would have chosen to approach Jesus at this time of day. Although we can't be sure, I wonder if, just as light and darkness are metaphors Jesus used to represent spiritual realities, the physical darkness Nicodemus traveled through to get to Jesus represents the spiritual darkness he was walking through in his personal life. Was he in a dark night of the soul? Had the shadows of doubt clouded his faith? Did he lack light in his life? Did the darkness represent confusion or a lack of understanding? If so, you and I can take comfort in this: We can come to Jesus in our own dark nights of the soul.

Even if we sneak around to get to his presence and do so without a lot of light in our lives, he will receive us anyway. And he will not just stay with us or embrace and dismiss our questions and doubts. Jesus illuminates the darkness—because he is the Light of the World.

PART 3

UNDERSTANDING

Now that we've finished a close reading of the Scriptures, we're going to spend some time on interpretation: doing our best to understand what God was saying to the original audience and what he's teaching us through the process. But to do so, we need to learn his ways and consider how God's Word would have been understood by the original audience before applying the same truths to our own lives. "Scripture interpretation" may sound a little stuffy, but understanding what God means to communicate to us in the Bible is crucial to enjoying a close relationship with Jesus. Part 3 will enable you to answer the question *What does it mean?*

I'VE SEEN LOTS OF MEMES on social media with the quote "Comparison is the thief of joy." When it comes to our personal lives, I agree. But in Bible study, comparison is the gift of clarity. What better way to understand what something means—or doesn't mean—than to compare it to something or someone else? As we study character types in Scripture, comparing people will be clarifying.

Take, for instance, the way John organizes his Gospel account of Jesus' life, death, and resurrection. He puts chapter 3 (the story of Nicodemus approaching Jesus in the dark of the night) next to a chapter about the Samaritan woman at the well (who encounters Jesus in the middle of the day).

Notice with me all the ways John's Gospel creates a literary comparison between Nicodemus and the woman at the well.

Nicodemus (John 3)	Woman at the Well (John 4)
Jewish	Samaritan
man	woman
high social status	low social status
formally trained in theology and the law	informally trained in the faith of the Samaritans
an authority figure	a powerless figure
met Jesus at night	encountered Jesus in the middle of the day
ended his conversation without an expression of faith	ended her conversation with an expression of faith

1. **How does this comparison of characters help you understand John's purpose in including Jesus' conversation with Nicodemus in his Gospel?**

These two strikingly different people were in two radically different places and had polar opposite responses in their first interactions with Christ—but both ended up as Christ followers. Their paths were different because they needed different things from Christ to believe. This should be good news to those of us whose spiritual journeys look very different from those of the other Christians in our lives. Your path may be different, but it's no less valid or worth sharing.

The literary structure of John's Gospel and the archetype of the Pharisees in the New Testament position someone like Nicodemus to be the foil in his story.

His example should encourage us to accept Jesus' truth, even when it challenges our status quo.

Nicodemus's meeting with Jesus is only one chapter of his story. Many chapters later, Nicodemus will show us that he has full faith in Christ. What started out as curiosity and some confusion led to courageous conviction. Nicodemus's journey has reminded me that my story is still being written. I'm still a work in progress. And maybe like Nicodemus, I, too, will enjoy new chapters in my faith story. Stories of my faith growing, my trust in Christ deepening, my hope expanding.

2. Which character do you relate to more: Nicodemus or the woman at the well? Why?

Whoever you relate to more, I want to remind you that Jesus went to the cross for people like you and me and Nicodemus and the woman at the well. Every single one of us.

MAKING CONNECTIONS

An important part of understanding the meaning of a Bible passage is getting a sense of its place in the broader storyline of Scripture. When we make connections between different parts of the Bible, we get a glimpse of the unity and cohesion of the Scriptures.

Here's one of the things I appreciate most about Nicodemus. Based on John 7, he was committed to hearing a person's testimony and evaluating his actions before making a judgment call. I think his commitment to research was part of the reason he approached Jesus with his questions in John 3. Nicodemus was keeping track of Jesus' claims and actions throughout his ministry on earth to try to determine whether Jesus was the Messiah. This is commendable.

After Jesus was on trial, after he was crucified, how did Nicodemus process all the information he'd been gathering about Jesus? What conclusion did he reach? That Jesus was the real deal.

One of the ways Nicodemus expressed his faith in Christ was anointing Jesus after his death. John 19 tells us that Nicodemus chose to be in Jerusalem on the day Jesus was crucified and stayed close enough to the events of the Crucifixion and connected enough to Jesus' disciples that he knew whom to go to and where to go to find Jesus.

3. Read John 19:38-42 and underline anything that has to do with Nicodemus.

[38] After this, Joseph of Arimathea, who was a disciple of Jesus—but secretly because of his fear of the Jews—asked Pilate that he might remove Jesus's body. Pilate gave him permission; so he came and took his body away. [39] Nicodemus (who had previously come to him at night) also came, bringing a mixture of about seventy-five pounds of myrrh and aloes. [40] They took Jesus's body and wrapped it in linen cloths with the fragrant spices, according to the burial custom of the Jews. [41] There was a garden in the place where he was crucified. A new tomb was in the garden; no one had yet been placed in it. [42] They placed Jesus there because of the Jewish day of preparation and since the tomb was nearby.

JOHN 19:38-42

4. Why do you think John made sure to include the parenthesis "(who had previously come to him at night)"?

Maybe John included the parenthesis "(who had previously come to him at night)" to create yet another comparison. It seems as if John wanted us to see that Nicodemus had finally accepted Jesus' words: that Jesus was the Light of the World.

5. If your story had made it into a Gospel, what would your parenthetical statement say about you? Would it be something like "Jim (who had previously rolled his eyes at Christians)" or "Heather (who had previously ignored God's nudges)"? Write it out below.

Faith in God changes everything. Whatever is in our parentheses is evidence that God is transforming our stories over time, and we would do well to celebrate the ways he makes us into something new.

✦ ✦ ✦

In every lesson, we will expand our storyline chart to include the character we are studying together.

THE SAINTS STORYLINE OF SCRIPTURE

Character	They represent . . .	How did they treat Jesus?
Nicodemus (John 3, 7, 19)	religious leaders who don't accept Jesus' teaching as the way of truth.	Nicodemus didn't accept Jesus' answers.
Judas (John 6, 12, 13, 18)	religious leaders who don't stay loyal to Jesus.	Judas betrayed Jesus.
Caiaphas (John 11, 18; Acts 4)	religious leaders who oppose the work of Christ and try to preserve power by any means necessary.	Caiaphas opposed Jesus.
Peter (John 18, 21)	religious leaders who deny Jesus with their words and actions when their reputations are on the line.	Peter denied Jesus.
Paul (Acts 8; 1 Timothy 1)	religious leaders who think the end justifies the means.	Paul persecuted Jesus.

What do we learn about Jesus?	Light and Darkness Imagery
Jesus tells the truth.	Nicodemus came to Jesus at night.
Jesus is loyal.	Judas betrayed Jesus at night.
Jesus can't be stopped.	Caiaphas's courtyard had a charcoal fire.
Jesus restores us.	Peter both denied Jesus and was restored by Jesus next to a charcoal fire.
Jesus transforms us.	Paul was blinded by a bright light.

1. **What about Nicodemus's story resonates with you most?**

2. **What did you learn about God's character in this lesson?**

3. **How should these truths shape your faith community and change you?**

RESPONDING

The purpose of Bible study is to help you become more Christlike; that's why part 4 will include journaling space for your reflection on and responses to the content and a blank checklist for actionable next steps. You'll be able to process what you're learning so that you can live out the concepts and pursue Christlikeness. Part 4 will enable you to answer the questions *What truths is this passage teaching?* and *How do I apply this to my life?*

AT FIRST, Nicodemus had a hard time accepting Jesus' testimony—that we all need to be "born again," that we need to have faith in Christ as our Savior. But Nicodemus was at least willing to do something about his faith questions. That takes courage. Because following Jesus is a lifelong journey of reconciling what we thought we knew about everything with the truth of God's Word. If that's you, you are courageous like Nicodemus. Keep bringing Jesus your questions. Even if you feel like you are in the dark, know this: Jesus wants to have a patient conversation with you.

Where Nicodemus went wrong was that he initially rejected Jesus' answers. He could have accepted Jesus' teachings as truth right away and experienced the goodness of being with Jesus when he walked on earth, but Nicodemus needed more time, more evidence, more testimony. If you can relate, know that your questions are not a barrier to your relationship. Do you remember how welcoming and patient Jesus was over the course of his ministry as he addressed people's concerns? Your Savior loves you even when you doubt or reject his truth.

1. STAY CURIOUS ABOUT YOUR ASSUMPTIONS.

Nicodemus's story issues a challenge to us all: Interrogate your assumptions. Nicodemus knew a lot about the coming Messiah. He was an expert in the law and deeply committed to the welfare of God's people. When Jesus started acting like a prophet, teaching with authority, and claiming to be God, Nicodemus brought his questions to the man himself. We can do the same. Jesus has the power to affirm or reorient our assumptions. Let's let him.

2. STAY CURIOUS ABOUT UNSETTLING VIEWS.

After Jesus told Nicodemus that he would have to be born again, Nicodemus could have shut down the conversation and walked away. Jesus' answer likely sounded like the ravings of a man who had lost his grip on reality. Instead, Nicodemus stayed in the conversation long enough to ask some clarifying questions—namely, *how?* Jesus was speaking metaphorically about a spiritual reality, but Nicodemus was trying to process his words literally. Nicodemus wanted to know how an adult could reenter their mother's womb to be born a second time, while Jesus wanted to teach Nicodemus that everyone—all God's chosen people, and even those who were not Jewish—could have access to the Kingdom of God if they would accept Jesus as the light in a dark world.

Nicodemus *came to Jesus at night* (3:2a), possibly because he was afraid of how some of his fellow leaders would react if they knew he had been talking to Jesus. However, it is also probable that in the symbolic world of this gospel, "night" is used to denote that Nicodemus was still in the darkness and had yet to embrace the light.[6]

Pratap C. Gine and Jacob Cherian, "John," in *South Asia Bible Commentary*

This must have been terribly unsettling for Nicodemus to process. But if you take only one thing away from Nicodemus's story, let it be the fact that he persevered to ask Jesus not just one question but several. And the text seems to imply that he was receptive enough to listen to Jesus' answers. Maybe that's your first step too. Bring your questions to Christ, and take time to really listen to Jesus' Word in the Gospel accounts.

Use this journaling space to process what you are learning.

Ask yourself how these truths impact your relationship with God and with others.

What is the Holy Spirit bringing to your mind as actionable next steps in your faith journey?

✦

✦

✦

REMAINING LOYAL TO JESUS WHEN YOU ARE TEMPTED TO BETRAY HIM

JUDAS:
THE DISCIPLE WHO SELLS JESUS OUT

SCRIPTURE: JOHN 6, 12, 13, 18

PART 1

CONTEXT

Before you begin your study, we will start with the context of the story we are about to read together: the setting, both cultural and historical; the people involved; and where our passage fits in the larger setting of Scripture. All these things help us make sense of what we're reading. Understanding the context of a Bible story is fundamental to reading Scripture well. Getting your bearings before you read will enable you to answer the question *What am I about to read?*

TED LASSO SWEPT THE EMMYS in 2021 and 2022. The popular TV show, about an American football coach leading a British soccer team, uses profanity like punctuation. But the show, which is the "most-nominated freshman comedy series in history,"[1] is also full of storylines that are heartfelt, relatable, and hilarious.

Jason Sudeikis plays the endlessly positive head coach, Ted Lasso, who is oblivious to the rules of soccer—something we might expect a head coach to have mastered. But Ted knows how to mold athletes into decent human beings on and off the field. He's a maker of men and a leader of leaders.

One of the many characters Ted Lasso catalyzes on the show is Nate, the underdeveloped and disrespected water boy. The thing is, Nate knows soccer well. And once Ted realizes Nate's potential, he gives him every opportunity to grow as a leader. Eventually Nate becomes one of the coaches.

Nate's character arc is a shining example of Ted Lasso's superpower: building up someone's skills and emotional fortitude.

For a time, Nate is the dark horse of the team—but then, sadly, his dark side begins to take over.

Nate is in Ted Lasso's inner circle by the end of the show's first season. They are friends, coworkers, and confidants. You get the sense that Ted's dream team always had a place for Nate; it just took a season to develop his character and to help him believe in himself, find his voice, and be his own man.

That's why when Nate betrays Ted Lasso, it's so excruciating to watch. Nate was privy to the most private aspects of Ted's life and knew his most tender vulnerabilities. You just never dreamed that Nate would turn his back on the one person who had believed in him, promoted him, and empowered him to flourish. It seems inconceivable for most of the season to think Nate would lash out at Ted Lasso. We're primed to expect loyalty for that kind of leadership.

Nate came to mind several times as I studied the life of Judas, the disciple of Jesus who betrayed his Savior and turned his back on his friends. Like all the characters we are studying together, Judas is complex. His presence in the Scriptures should make us all feel some tension. Judas was in Jesus' inner circle. He likely listened to many of Jesus' sermons, healed people alongside the other disciples, and enjoyed the fellowship of Jesus and his closest friends.

But as we will see, something had been stirring in Judas for a long time. Something evil. You'll notice in the Bible readings that many things contributed to Judas's handing Jesus over to the authorities who wanted to crucify him. Judas was greedy, *and* the enemy was tempting him to sell Jesus out.

Although the phenomenon of abandoning an initial interest or faith in Jesus was surely to be found in Jesus' own day, there is in the Gospel of John a particular horror of disciples who fall away from or desert Jesus, hand him over to the authorities, or otherwise fail to persevere in their allegiance to him.[2]

Marianne Meye Thompson, *John: A Commentary*

What you are about to read is a story of a disciple who didn't remain loyal to Jesus. His story is tragic. But you're also going to find glimmers of hope in Judas's story.

Judas is mentioned in all four Gospels: Matthew, Mark, Luke, and John. But for our purposes, we are only going to focus on what we find about Judas in John's Gospel. John shapes his narrative biography of Jesus' life, death, and resurrection to show us that Jesus is God and that his disciples are a key element of bringing the Kingdom of God to earth.

John mentions Judas a lot in his Gospel. I wish we had time to read every mention, but we're going to focus on two episodes of Judas's story. Before we do, though, we'll need some context about Judas from John's perspective.

Judas was a common name in Jesus' day and can also be translated Judah or Jude.[3] Our focus will be on Judas Iscariot. This Judas was the son of someone named Simon and was one of the twelve disciples chosen by Jesus to be part of his inner circle. Jesus had many more than twelve disciples. For instance, he had several female disciples: Mary Magdalene, Mary and Martha of Bethany, and Susanna, to name a few. But the number in the inner circle has a literary function: It represents Israel's twelve tribes from the Old Testament.[4]

John made sure to include some important details that give us more perspective about Judas. For example, Judas had prime opportunities to abandon Jesus early on in Jesus' earthly ministry, but he didn't. In John 6, Jesus said something that angered some of his disciples, and many of them turned away from Christ and left the fold. But Judas stayed. You could read this ominously, as if the evil in Judas was determined to wait for an opportune time to take Jesus down. Or it simply could be that Judas didn't have any ill will in his heart at this point in the story.

John also made sure to tell a story about Judas getting angry with a fellow disciple, Mary of Bethany (John 12). Mary anointed Jesus' feet with expensive perfume, and since Judas was a thief, secretly stealing from the group's shared funds, he was angry. To Judas, Mary's extravagant display of devotion was sheer waste. By the time we get to the foot-washing scene in John 13, we know several things about Judas: He was a disciple, he was greedy, he was a thief, and Jesus knew all along that Judas would betray him.

Judas epitomizes those who have fallen away: if they had once believed in Jesus, they do so no longer. Judas thus stands in contrast to Mary: she spends generously what she has to honor Jesus, while Judas greedily grasps what does not belong to him. Mary honors Jesus; Judas betrays him.[5]

Marianne Meye Thompson, *John: A Commentary*

If you know the sting of betrayal, you are going to find solidarity with Christ in this lesson. He knows what you've been through. Your Savior is attuned to your struggles and your needs. He is committed to you. Jesus intentionally experienced the same. He is a safe person.

And for those of us who have been the betrayer, I think you, too, will find encouragement in this lesson. Jesus knew all along that Judas would abandon him. But he welcomed him into his inner circle, journeyed with him for years during his earthly ministry, and did not lash out when his life was on the line. Your Savior loves you no matter what. Like Judas, you will likely experience hard consequences for your sin, but please don't forget: Jesus always calls you back. And as you pursue repentance, he is always ready to welcome you in.

Judas's story is a cautionary tale for anyone who considers themself a Christ follower. Remaining loyal to Jesus is not a given. Together, we can learn from Judas's mistakes and choose steadfast fidelity to Christ.

1. **PERSONAL CONTEXT: What is going on in your life right now that might impact how you understand this Bible character?**

2. **SPIRITUAL CONTEXT: If you've never studied this Bible character before, what piques your curiosity? If you've studied this character before, what impressions and insights do you recall?**

PART 2

SEEING

Seeing the text is vital if we want the heart of the Scripture passage to sink in. We read slowly and intentionally through the text with the context in mind. As we practice close, thoughtful reading of Scripture, we pick up on phrases, implications, and meanings we might otherwise have missed. Part 2 includes close Scripture reading and observation questions to empower you to answer the question *What is the story saying?*

1. **Read John 13:1-30 and underline every reference to Judas.**

13 Now before the Feast of the Passover, Jesus, knowing that His hour had come that He would depart from this world to the Father, having loved His own who were in the world, He loved them to the end. ² And during supper, the devil having already put into the heart of Judas Iscariot, the son of Simon, to betray Him, ³ Jesus, knowing that the Father had handed all things over to Him, and that He had come forth from God and was going back to God, ⁴ got up from supper and laid His outer garments aside; and He took a towel and tied it around Himself.

⁵ Then He poured water into the basin, and began washing the disciples' feet and wiping them with the towel which He had tied around Himself. ⁶ So He came to Simon Peter. He said to Him, "Lord, You are

washing my feet?" 7 Jesus answered and said to him, "What I am doing, you do not realize right now, but you will understand later." 8 Peter said to Him, "Never shall You wash my feet!" Jesus answered him, "If I do not wash you, you have no place with Me." 9 Simon Peter said to Him, "Lord, then wash not only my feet, but also my hands and my head!" 10 Jesus said to him, "He who has bathed needs only to wash his feet; otherwise he is completely clean. And you are clean—but not all of you." 11 For He knew the one who was betraying Him; it was for this reason that He said, "Not all of you are clean."

12 Then, when He had washed their feet, and taken His garments and reclined at the table again, He said to them, "Do you know what I have done for you? 13 You call Me 'Teacher' and 'Lord'; and you are correct, for so I am. 14 So if I, the Lord and the Teacher, washed your feet, you also ought to wash one another's feet. 15 For I gave you an example, so that you also would do just as I did for you. 16 Truly, truly I say to you, a slave is not greater than his master, nor is one who is sent greater than the one who sent him. 17 If you know these things, you are blessed if you do them. 18 I am not speaking about all of you. I know the ones whom I have chosen; but this is happening so that the Scripture may be fulfilled, 'HE WHO EATS MY BREAD HAS LIFTED UP HIS HEEL AGAINST ME.' 19 From now on I am telling you before it happens, so that when it does happen, you may believe that I am He. 20 Truly, truly I say to you, the one who receives anyone I send, receives Me; and the one who receives Me receives Him who sent Me."

21 When Jesus had said these things, He became troubled in spirit, and testified and said, "Truly, truly I say to you that one of you will betray Me." 22 The disciples began looking at one another, at a loss to know of which one He was speaking. 23 Lying back on Jesus' chest was one of His disciples, whom Jesus loved. 24 So Simon Peter nodded to this disciple and said to him, "Tell us who it is of whom He is speaking." 25 He then simply leaned back on Jesus' chest and said to Him, "Lord, who is it?" 26 Jesus then answered, "That man is the one for whom I shall dip the piece of

bread and give it to him." So when He had dipped the piece of bread, He took and gave it to Judas, the son of Simon Iscariot. ²⁷ After this, Satan then entered him. Therefore Jesus said to him, "What you are doing, do it quickly." ²⁸ Now none of those reclining at the table knew for what purpose He had said this to him. ²⁹ For some were assuming, since Judas kept the money box, that Jesus was saying to him, "Buy the things we need for the feast"; or else, that he was to give something to the poor. ³⁰ So after receiving the piece of bread, he left immediately; and it was night.

JOHN 13:1-30, NASB

2. Who is credited with planting betrayal in Judas's heart? (See John 13:2.)

The devil's role in Judas's betrayal does not absolve Judas of guilt. Greed had been festering in his life, and he had been stealing from Jesus and his disciples. Both the devil and Judas were responsible for his actions. But the Scriptures are explicit: Jesus knew this was coming and willingly laid down his life.

3. Why did Jesus reveal to his disciples that someone would betray him (John 13:19)?

4. How did Jesus feel about the things that would soon happen and about Judas's role in them (John 13:21)?

5. How would you describe what happened to Judas in John 13:27?

John mentions that as Judas left the disciples, it was night. The lights had gone out on Judas. He walked away from his Savior in darkness. The scenery symbolizes the spiritual darkness that had entered Judas through the physical darkness he was entering himself.

By leaving, Judas likely missed what many scholars refer to as the "upper-room discourse," a long sermon Jesus gave to his disciples. Here are some of the points Judas missed from Jesus' sermon:

+ As a disciple, don't let your heart be troubled.
+ The Holy Spirit would be the Great Counselor after Jesus' death.
+ The Holy Spirit would be the great teacher of truth after Jesus' death.
+ Nothing worth doing can be done apart from Christ.

All things Judas needed to hear. But instead, the next time Judas shows up in the storyline, he is handing Jesus over to an angry mob.

6. **Read John 18:1-5 and underline anything that refers to Judas.**

18 When Jesus had spoken these words, He went away with His disciples across the ravine of the Kidron, where there was a garden which He entered with His disciples. ² Now Judas, who was betraying Him, also knew the place, because Jesus had often met there with His disciples. ³ So Judas, having obtained the Roman cohort and officers from the chief priests and the Pharisees, came there with lanterns, torches, and weapons. ⁴ Jesus therefore, knowing all the things that were coming upon Him, came out into the open and said to them, "Whom are you seeking?" ⁵ They answered Him, "Jesus the Nazarene." He said to them, "I am He." And Judas also, who was betraying Him, was standing with them.

JOHN 18:1-5, NASB

7. **Write out John 18:2 below:**

8. **Where was Judas standing? (See John 18:5.)**

Physically and metaphorically, Judas had switched sides. He'd moved away from Christ.

My first thought after reading this story is *Where do I stand with Jesus?* Maybe you're asking yourself the same question: *Where do I stand with Jesus?*

Are we standing with Jesus or against him? No matter how you answer that question, take heart. Even in the middle of betrayal, Jesus did not allow his loyal disciples to harm Judas. After all, Jesus had just taught his disciples to love one another. When Judas showed no love to Jesus, Jesus still offered love to Judas, and he trained his disciples to do the same. *This* is good news.

PART 3

UNDERSTANDING

Now that we've finished a close reading of the Scriptures, we're going to spend some time on interpretation: doing our best to understand what God was saying to the original audience and what he's teaching us through the process. But to do so, we need to learn his ways and consider how God's Word would have been understood by the original audience before applying the same truths to our own lives. "Scripture interpretation" may sound a little stuffy, but understanding what God means to communicate to us in the Bible is crucial to enjoying a close relationship with Jesus. Part 3 will enable you to answer the question *What does it mean?*

FLIP WILSON WAS the first Black entertainer to host a successful weekly variety show on network television.[6] He became wildly popular after regular appearances on *The Ed Sullivan Show* impersonating made-up characters like Reverend Leroy. Reverend Leroy fictitiously pastored the Church of What's Happenin' Now and had many conversations with a member of his congregation, Geraldine Jones. It was through those hilarious characters that Wilson coined the saying "The devil made me do it."[7] Flip's stand-up comedy made light of something many of us might be tempted to do: shift the blame for our sin onto the devil. But I think we would all agree that sin is no laughing matter. And reducing our behavior to the enemy's influence can be a cop-out.

For Flip Wilson's character Miss Geraldine, the devil alone was responsible for frivolous purchases like expensive dresses. Her excuse was that the devil made her do it. The phrase came to mind as I studied Judas's story. Flip Wilson's jokes about the devil's influence on our decisions are funny, and they place all the blame on the devil. In contrast, the Bible presents Judas's sin as having dual influence.

1. **What does Judas's story teach you about the nature of sin and the complex causes of evil?**

I find it illuminating that Judas's sin and the devil's temptation worked in tandem. Judas was responsible, *and* the devil was responsible too. We know that God works all things together for the good of those who love him (Romans 8:28). That God is not the author of evil. But neither was God surprised by Judas's evil behavior.

2. **What does Judas's story teach about being loyal to Christ?**

Judas's defection from the ranks of Jesus' disciples and his handing over of Jesus are two sides of one coin: what Judas does, he does not as a disciple, but as one who has ceased to follow Jesus and has been lured away from faithful discipleship.[8]

Marianne Meye Thompson, *John: A Commentary*

As I journeyed through these Scripture texts, I was a bit on edge. I've still got lingering questions about how Judas could have been in Jesus' orbit, close enough to be one of the twelve disciples, and still sell Jesus out. How did this happen? What led Judas to this tragic end? And could I be capable of something like this? Will I ever turn away from Christ?

And maybe that is the reason God included Judas's story in the storyline of Scripture. Judas is an archetypal character representing those who should be faithful to Christ and aren't. If there is anything I'm taking away from this story about loyalty, it is that we are all susceptible to temptation—and we'd better make it our business to stay loyal to Jesus.

MAKING CONNECTIONS

An important part of understanding the meaning of a Bible passage is getting a sense of its place in the broader storyline of Scripture. When we make connections between different parts of the Bible, we get a glimpse of the unity and cohesion of the Scriptures.

One of the common translations of Judas's name is Judah. And I believe that Judas's story in the New Testament has some echoes of Judah's story all the way back in Genesis 37.

The book of Genesis is about our beginnings, how God created the world and people to enjoy his presence. God chose one family to be a blessing to all people, and most of the book of Genesis follows this family through the ages. One family member, Joseph, is an oversharer and a little prideful, too. He gets under his older brothers' skin enough to make them want to kill him. (Yes, the book of Genesis is better than any TV drama ever.)

As Joseph's brothers plot to kill him, Judah speaks up.

3. **Read Genesis 37:18-28 and underline anything that references Judah.**

¹⁸ When [Joseph's brothers] saw [Joseph] from a distance, and before he came closer to them, they plotted against him to put him to death. ¹⁹ They

said to one another, "Here comes this dreamer! 20 Now then, come and let's kill him, and throw him into one of the pits; and we will say, 'A vicious animal devoured him.' Then we will see what will become of his dreams!" 21 But Reuben heard this and rescued him out of their hands by saying, "Let's not take his life." 22 Then Reuben said to them, "Shed no blood. Throw him into this pit that is in the wilderness, but do not lay a hand on him"—so that later he might rescue him out of their hands, to return him to his father. 23 So it came about, when Joseph reached his brothers, that they stripped Joseph of his tunic, the multicolored tunic that was on him; 24 and they took him and threw him into the pit. Now the pit was empty, without any water in it.

25 Then they sat down to eat a meal. But as they raised their eyes and looked, behold, a caravan of Ishmaelites was coming from Gilead, with their camels carrying labdanum resin, balsam, and myrrh, on their way to bring them down to Egypt. 26 And Judah said to his brothers, "What profit is it for us to kill our brother and cover up his blood? 27 Come, and let's sell him to the Ishmaelites and not lay our hands on him, for he is our brother, our own flesh." And his brothers listened to him. 28 Then some Midianite traders passed by, so they pulled him out and lifted Joseph out of the pit, and sold him to the Ishmaelites for twenty shekels of silver. So they brought Joseph into Egypt.

GENESIS 37:18-28, NASB

4. In your own words, summarize what Judah proposed to his brothers (Genesis 37:26-27).

5. **Compare Judah's story in Genesis 37 to Judas's story in John 18. What similarities do you see between these two characters? What differences do you notice?**

Similarities:

✦

✦

✦

Differences:

✦

✦

✦

Judah and Judas were both willing to betray someone they should have loved and delegate the dirty work to others. Both men acted cowardly, and both seemed to be in it for the money. I don't want to overemphasize the role money played in both Judah's and Judas's stories, but it's still worth noticing this detail. When Jesus talked about our hearts being in the same place as our earthly treasures (Matthew 6:21), he was right. *Follow the money* seems appropriate for this storyline of betrayal.

✦ ✦ ✦

Let's check back in on our Saints Storyline.

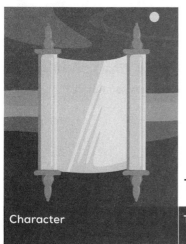

THE SAINTS STORYLINE OF SCRIPTURE

Character	They represent . . .	How did they treat Jesus?
Nicodemus (John 3, 7, 19)	religious leaders who don't accept Jesus' teaching as the way of truth.	Nicodemus didn't accept Jesus' answers.
Judas (John 6, 12, 13, 18)	religious leaders who don't stay loyal to Jesus.	Judas betrayed Jesus.
Caiaphas (John 11, 18; Acts 4)	religious leaders who oppose the work of Christ and try to preserve power by any means necessary.	Caiaphas opposed Jesus.
Peter (John 18, 21)	religious leaders who deny Jesus with their words and actions when their reputations are on the line.	Peter denied Jesus.
Paul (Acts 8; 1 Timothy 1)	religious leaders who think the end justifies the means.	Paul persecuted Jesus.

What do we learn about Jesus?	Light and Darkness Imagery
Jesus tells the truth.	Nicodemus came to Jesus at night.
Jesus is loyal.	Judas betrayed Jesus at night.
Jesus can't be stopped.	Caiaphas's courtyard had a charcoal fire.
Jesus restores us.	Peter both denied Jesus and was restored by Jesus next to a charcoal fire.
Jesus transforms us.	Paul was blinded by a bright light.

1. **What about Judas's story resonates with you most?**

2. **What did you learn about God's character in this lesson?**

3. **How should these truths shape your faith community and change you?**

RESPONDING

The purpose of Bible study is to help you become more Christlike; that's why part 4 will include journaling space for your reflection on and responses to the content and a blank checklist for actionable next steps. You'll be able to process what you're learning so that you can live out the concepts and pursue Christlikeness. Part 4 will enable you to answer the questions *What truths is this passage teaching?* and *How do I apply this to my life?*

JUDAS LEFT HIS PLACE in Jesus' inner circle to stand on the sidelines with an angry mob. And for what? Matthew's Gospel tells us that Judas sold Jesus out for only thirty pieces of silver (Matthew 26:14-16). It might be tempting to write off Judas as an extreme example of apostasy, but I find myself deeply troubled by Judas's proximity to Jesus and his willingness to give up. He went from being in the trusted inner circle to being a disloyal outsider.

All I want—and I suspect all you want—is to remain loyal to Jesus. He is my everything.

In *Ted Lasso*, a character named Dani Rojas loves to yell, "Football is life!" And that is how I feel about Jesus. Jesus is life! But did Judas feel that way at one time too? Did he move from *all-in* to *satisfied* to *let's pocket some profit*—in exchange for a place with Jesus?

As I ruminated on Judas's story and how you and I can stay loyal to Jesus, two reflection points came to mind.

1. NOTICE YOUR REACTIONS.

Judas couldn't stand that Mary of Bethany wanted to pour out all her expensive perfume to anoint Jesus' feet for burial. He just couldn't abide someone else's generosity, devotion, and tenderness. Moreover, Judas felt entitled to steal from the disciples' shared purse, using his responsibility to keep the coins as an excuse to get what he thought he deserved. In both cases, Judas reacted greedily. Judas's reactions should lead us to a couple of questions: *How do we react when someone else is getting what we think we deserve? And how far will we go to get it?*

Our reactions are revealing. We can pay attention to our reactions by writing down how we respond when we don't get our way. Because beneath those reactions is a whole host of beliefs driving our behavior. And we need to take an inventory so we can root out where the enemy is at work.

2. QUESTION YOUR MOTIVES.

Judas was motivated by money. And his greed ultimately took him to the darkest places of guilt and regret that a person can go (Matthew 27:3-5). You and I don't have to suffer that same fate. We can choose to interrogate our inclinations now. *What motivates us? What keeps us going?* Assigning motives to our behavior could help us all uncover what is going on underneath the surface.

Whatever holds our attention and tempts us to make bad choices needs to be replaced with unyielding, ongoing adoration for Jesus. He can be our motivation. Our everything.

I wonder what Judas's life would have looked like if he'd heeded Jesus' words in John 12:7: "Leave her alone." I wonder if Jesus was saying more to Judas than just to leave Mary of Bethany alone. What if Jesus was also talking about the motive underneath Judas's reaction—his greed?

Whatever unhealthy thing drives you—leave that motive alone.

Use this journaling space to process what you are learning.

Ask yourself how these truths impact your relationship with God and with others.

What is the Holy Spirit bringing to your mind as actionable next steps in your faith journey?

+

+

+

USING YOUR INFLUENCE FOR GOOD WHEN IT DOESN'T BENEFIT YOU

CAIAPHAS:
THE HIGH PRIEST WHO PROTECTS HIS POWER

SCRIPTURE: JOHN 11, 18; ACTS 4

PART 1

CONTEXT

Before you begin your study, we will start with the context of the story we are about to read together: the setting, both cultural and historical; the people involved; and where our passage fits in the larger setting of Scripture. All these things help us make sense of what we're reading. Understanding the context of a Bible story is fundamental to reading Scripture well. Getting your bearings before you read will enable you to answer the question What am I about to read?

MARY AND MARTHA OF BETHANY were remarkable disciples of Jesus. The sisters were devastated when their beloved brother, Lazarus, died (John 11). Who wouldn't be? Almost nothing is worse than surviving the death of a sibling. But what Mary and Martha faced *after* Lazarus's death deepened their grief: the confusing, seemingly callous absence of Jesus when their family needed him most. You see, Mary, Martha, Lazarus, and Jesus were all really good friends.

Death didn't have the final word in Lazarus's story, though. Resurrection did.

Jesus came later than expected, but he came nonetheless. And he raised Lazarus from the dead. To the relief of the sisters and to the shock of everyone who saw it, Lazarus walked out of his grave.

Lazarus's resurrection story, with his untimely death and Jesus' late arrival, is all about timing. In the midst of all this, Martha affirmed Jesus as the Messiah (John 11:27)—and she did so while Lazarus still lay in the grave. The timing of her profession of faith was a radical expression of her confidence in Jesus. Even as her brother lay lifeless in his grave, Martha still believed Jesus was the Christ.

What had escaped the imagination of many Jewish leaders Martha seemed to have understood: Jesus is exactly who he said he was.

I bring up this pivotal scene because it's the context for the character we will study in this lesson: Caiaphas, the high priest. In John's Gospel, we meet Caiaphas for the first time after some Jews report Lazarus's resurrection to the Pharisees (John 11:46). Lazarus dies. Martha proclaims Jesus as the Messiah. Jesus raises Lazarus from the dead. And then some Jews report the resurrection miracle to the religious authorities. The news reaches Caiaphas, the high priest.

> The Jewish elite had worked out a system that benefitted both them and their Roman overlords. However, Jewish nationhood and the power base of the elite would be in danger if the Romans were forced to act.[2]
>
> Pratap C. Gine and Jacob Cherian, "John," in *South Asia Bible Commentary*

High priests were set apart even from other religious leaders by some special requirements, including not going anywhere near a corpse.[1] In addition to serving in the Temple rituals, high priests interpreted the Hebrew Scriptures and announced oracles. The Roman government, which ruled over Judea during Jesus' earthly ministry, relied on the high priests to keep the peace and maintain order among the Jews. As high priest, Caiaphas had social status among the Jews, authority at the Temple, and a place among the Sanhedrin—the governing council of Jewish leaders—which meant political power.[3]

Caiaphas could have responded to Jesus' miracles the way Martha of Bethany had—with rejoicing. Instead, he reverted to what I think most of us have tried before: denial.

Caiaphas is an example of what happens when we let love of power—or fear of losing it—drive our decisions. But within his story we see that earthly power never gets the final say. If we're scared of losing control, scared of releasing what power we have, we can remember the truth that we have nothing to lose and nothing to fear.

As you read Caiaphas's story, you are about to see the unstoppable, undeniable love of Jesus. You're about to see just how committed Jesus is to your freedom. Neither a corrupt political system nor a corrupt religious system can keep Jesus from offering his life for yours and mine.

1. **PERSONAL CONTEXT: What is going on in your life right now that might impact how you understand this Bible character?**

2. **SPIRITUAL CONTEXT: If you've never studied this Bible character before, what piques your curiosity? If you've studied this character before, what impressions and insights do you recall?**

SEEING

Seeing the text is vital if we want the heart of the Scripture passage to sink in. We read slowly and intentionally through the text with the context in mind. As we practice close, thoughtful reading of Scripture, we pick up on phrases, implications, and meanings we might otherwise have missed. Part 2 includes close Scripture reading and observation questions to empower you to answer the question *What is the story saying?*

1. **Read John 11:38-57 and underline everything Caiaphas said.**

³⁸ Then Jesus, deeply moved again, came to the tomb. It was a cave, and a stone was lying against it. ³⁹ "Remove the stone," Jesus said.

Martha, the dead man's sister, told him, "Lord, there is already a stench because he has been dead four days."

⁴⁰ Jesus said to her, "Didn't I tell you that if you believed you would see the glory of God?"

⁴¹ So they removed the stone. Then Jesus raised his eyes and said, "Father, I thank you that you heard me. ⁴² I know that you always hear me, but because of the crowd standing here I said this, so that they may believe you sent me." ⁴³ After he said this, he shouted with a loud voice, "Lazarus, come out!" ⁴⁴ The dead man came out bound hand and foot

with linen strips and with his face wrapped in a cloth. Jesus said to them, "Unwrap him and let him go."

⁴⁵ Therefore, many of the Jews who came to Mary and saw what he did believed in him. ⁴⁶ But some of them went to the Pharisees and told them what Jesus had done.

⁴⁷ So the chief priests and the Pharisees convened the Sanhedrin and were saying, "What are we going to do since this man is doing many signs? ⁴⁸ If we let him go on like this, everyone will believe in him, and the Romans will come and take away both our place and our nation."

⁴⁹ One of them, Caiaphas, who was high priest that year, said to them, "You know nothing at all! ⁵⁰ You're not considering that it is to your advantage that one man should die for the people rather than the whole nation perish." ⁵¹ He did not say this on his own, but being high priest that year he prophesied that Jesus was going to die for the nation, ⁵² and not for the nation only, but also to unite the scattered children of God. ⁵³ So from that day on they plotted to kill him.

⁵⁴ Jesus therefore no longer walked openly among the Jews but departed from there to the countryside near the wilderness, to a town called Ephraim, and he stayed there with the disciples.

⁵⁵ Now the Jewish Passover was near, and many went up to Jerusalem from the country to purify themselves before the Passover. ⁵⁶ They were looking for Jesus and asking one another as they stood in the temple, "What do you think? He won't come to the festival, will he?" ⁵⁷ The chief priests and the Pharisees had given orders that if anyone knew where he was, he should report it so that they could arrest him.

JOHN 11:38-57

2. **Lazarus's resurrection caused quite the stir. Some of the Jewish people who'd witnessed the resurrection and heard Mary and Martha's testimony went running to the chief priests and Pharisees. After these people reported the miracle, the governing council for the Jews, the Sanhedrin, convened. Write out what you imagine the minutes for this meeting might have included.**

MEETING MINUTES

    Date:

    Sanhedrin Leaders Present:

    Meeting Minutes:

3. **The role of the chief priests was to protect the Jewish people—and Jesus was healing and resurrecting those most in need of protection. How did the chief priests respond to the signs and wonders of Jesus? They were . . .**

   ☐ thankful someone was healing and resurrecting their people
   ☐ joyful that Lazarus was back to life after death
   ☐ curious about how Jesus' ministry fit into their faith
   ☐ scared

4. List all three fears the voting members of the Sanhedrin mention in John 11:48:

1.

2.

3.

Not only did their fears provide an ominous motive for murder, but their response also completely lacked any celebration over Lazarus's resurrection. For leaders who claimed to fear for their people's safety, they didn't seem overwhelmed with joy that Jesus was delivering their people from death.

5. What opportunity did Caiaphas see in their situation?

But while Caiaphas is willing to hand Jesus over to death, he is apparently not willing to sacrifice himself.[4]

Marianne Meye Thompson,
John: A Commentary

Perhaps this is one of John's points in Caiaphas's story. The high priest was quick to find an angle that both preserved the relative security of the Jewish nation and maintained his seat of authority. Power can do that to us, too—inflate our sense of importance and make us think we're the ones holding everything together. If we're not careful, we, like Caiaphas, can forget that it's God's job (and for God's glory) to save his people.

Many in the Sanhedrin seemed worried that Jesus and his growing popularity would take the whole Jewish community down. But Caiaphas was sure that Jesus would take all the blame for causing confusion and disruption among the Jews. On this point, Caiaphas was absolutely correct. But in his other assumption, he was completely wrong. Caiaphas believed that Jesus' death would be the end of the movement Jesus had started. He had no idea that Jesus' death would only be the beginning.

6. How did the Sanhedrin plot to solve their problem and ease their fears? (See John 11:53.)

7. Where did Jesus and his disciples go when he left Jerusalem? (See John 11:54.)

Notice with me the fork in the road as this scene ends. Caiaphas and the others stayed in Jerusalem for the Passover, and Jesus left to go to the countryside, "near the wilderness" (John 11:54).

The buzzing city of Jerusalem represents the rulers and leaders of all the governing bodies, religious and political. But the wilderness is where God's people had been exiled. It is where they had escaped the tyranny of the Egyptian pharaoh and where their faith had been tested.

I wonder if John wants us to picture Jesus and Caiaphas going separate ways, opposite directions, so that we can understand what was happening to Caiaphas internally. Caiaphas was turning away from God. He was taking sides. And what we will see next is that Caiaphas didn't just side with Jesus' antagonizers—Caiaphas chose to side with himself.

8. Jesus wasn't the only person the Sanhedrin were plotting to kill. Based on John 12:9–11, who else did they need to murder to bury evidence of Jesus' power?

Caiaphas's part in this story is particularly dark. The role of high priest was meant to be a position of authority over and service to God's people. What did he do with this influence? He positioned himself in opposition to Jesus and in opposition to the values of the Torah. This is not a story about the evils of Judaism. This is a story about a man who, though commissioned and anointed to serve his people through justice and mercy, showed neither.

Any one of us who follows Jesus has struggled to reconcile the truth about Jesus with our preconceived notions of faith. But Caiaphas embodies what happens if we choose not to believe Jesus even after we are confronted with the reality of who he is and what he has done.

PART 3

UNDERSTANDING

Now that we've finished a close reading of the Scriptures, we're going to spend some time on interpretation: doing our best to understand what God was saying to the original audience and what he's teaching us through the process. But to do so, we need to learn his ways and consider how God's Word would have been understood by the original audience before applying the same truths to our own lives. "Scripture interpretation" may sound a little stuffy, but understanding what God means to communicate to us in the Bible is crucial to enjoying a close relationship with Jesus. Part 3 will enable you to answer the question *What does it mean?*

HAVE YOU EVER HAD a favorite teacher? Mine was my high-school music teacher, Mrs. Crenshaw. I knew she loved me. She taught me plenty about music, but what I remember most is how she always greeted me with a smile and seemed to delight in our conversations. Everything she had to say, I listened to. Everything she asked of us, I tried to obey. She likely had more influence in my teenage life than anyone besides my parents.

Much like Mrs. Crenshaw impacted my life, Caiaphas held a place of influence and importance with all the Jewish people. When he voted in the Sanhedrin or voiced his opinion, people listened. And his views carried clout with the Romans, too.

The significance of Caiaphas's voice is why we need to notice how John sets up his Gospel. John doesn't highlight Caiaphas's impact or clout. He zooms in on his leadership failures.

Caiaphas did not steward his influence in a way that brought God glory, protected his people, or honored the Torah. Somewhere along the way, his political ambitions and self-protective instincts kept him from recognizing—and led him to opposing—God in the flesh. Corruption is a temptation for all of us. How can we diagnose whether we are choosing the wrong side? We need to check whether we are going against Jesus.

At first, Caiaphas looked for the strategic advantage: How would Jesus' demise help the Jewish people? Then his complicity turned into silence. John 18:12–19:16 summarizes Caiaphas's role in Jesus' arrest, in his trials before the governing bodies, and ultimately in his crucifixion. At every point, Caiaphas had the opportunity to do the right thing—to speak up or resist the decisions being made. But he didn't.

Greed may have motivated Judas to betray Jesus, but it seems that power is what blinded Caiaphas.

Soon after Jesus' resurrection and ascension, Jesus' followers started a movement to make disciples—healing and teaching in the same way Jesus had when he'd been on earth. And sometimes Jesus' disciples faced persecution when they preached and healed in his name.

One example is in the book of Acts. Luke reports a story in which Peter and John had just gotten in trouble with the Sanhedrin for healing a lame man in the name of Christ. Caiaphas and several other priests threw Peter and John in jail in hopes they could stop the message of Jesus' resurrection from getting out. Sounds familiar, doesn't it? Caiaphas tried to stop Jesus from preaching and healing before Jesus' crucifixion, and then he tried to stop Jesus' disciples from preaching and healing after Jesus' resurrection.

1. **Read Acts 4:1-22. After reading the passage, write out what you imagine the meeting minutes might have been from the Sanhedrin's discussion about Peter and John's ministry.**

4 While they were speaking to the people, the priests, the captain of the temple police, and the Sadducees confronted them, ² because they were annoyed that they were teaching the people and proclaiming in Jesus the resurrection of the dead. ³ So they seized them and took them into custody until the next day since it was already evening. ⁴ But many of those who heard the message believed, and the number of the men came to about five thousand.

⁵ The next day, their rulers, elders, and scribes assembled in Jerusalem ⁶ with Annas the high priest, Caiaphas, John, Alexander, and all the members of the high-priestly family. ⁷ After they had Peter and John stand before them, they began to question them: "By what power or in what name have you done this?"

⁸ Then Peter was filled with the Holy Spirit and said to them, "Rulers of the people and elders: ⁹ If we are being examined today about a good deed done to a disabled man, by what means he was healed, ¹⁰ let it be known to all of you and to all the people of Israel, that by the name of Jesus Christ of Nazareth, whom you crucified and whom God raised from the dead— by him this man is standing here before you healthy. ¹¹ This Jesus is

the stone rejected by you builders,
which has become the cornerstone.

¹² There is salvation in no one else, for there is no other name under heaven given to people by which we must be saved."

¹³ When they observed the boldness of Peter and John and realized that they were uneducated and untrained men, they were amazed and recognized that they had been with Jesus. ¹⁴ And since they saw the man who had been healed standing with them, they had nothing to say in opposition. ¹⁵ After they ordered them to leave the Sanhedrin, they conferred among themselves, ¹⁶ saying, "What should we do with these men? For an obvious sign has been done through them, clear to everyone living in Jerusalem, and we cannot deny it. ¹⁷ But so that this does not spread any further among the people, let's threaten them against speaking to anyone in this name again." ¹⁸ So they called for them and ordered them not to speak or teach at all in the name of Jesus.

¹⁹ Peter and John answered them, "Whether it's right in the sight of God for us to listen to you rather than to God, you decide; ²⁰ for we are unable to stop speaking about what we have seen and heard."

²¹ After threatening them further, they released them. They found no way to punish them because the people were all giving glory to God over what had been done. ²² For this sign of healing had been performed on a man over forty years old.

ACTS 4:1-22

MEETING MINUTES

    Date:

    Sanhedrin Leaders Present:

    Meeting Minutes:

2. Why did the Jerusalem council feel compelled to do something about Peter and John? (See Acts 4:16.)

The Sanhedrin couldn't deny that Jesus, and now his disciples, had the power to heal—so they tried burying the story. The joke was on them. Resurrection by its nature unburies everyone.

Caiaphas had yet another opportunity to side with Jesus, to use his influence for good, to accept reality. He could have repented and believed and joined the Jesus movement. Instead, he doubled down. Denying Jesus when denial is no longer possible is a tragedy. We should feel the tension in the text as we watch Caiaphas reject yet another opportunity to choose the way of Christ. While Caiaphas had a death grip on his place in the Jewish community, the church of Jesus was being unleashed by the hand of God himself.

3. What did Peter and John cite as their reasons for not staying quiet about Jesus? (See Acts 4:19-20.)

Not only did Peter and John grow bolder in their proclamations of the gospel, but this conversation between Peter, John, Caiaphas, and the other priests birthed a revival among Jesus' followers through these prayers:

> [Peter and John prayed,] 29 "And now, Lord, consider their threats, and grant that your servants may speak your word with all boldness, 30 while you stretch out your hand for healing, and signs and wonders are performed through the name of your holy servant Jesus." 31 When they had prayed, the place where they were assembled was shaken, and they were all filled with the Holy Spirit and began to speak the word of God boldly.
>
> ACTS 4:29-31

4. **Why do you think Jesus' followers grew bolder and more confident in sharing the gospel after this moment?**

5. **How bold and confident are you when sharing your faith with others?**

What happened was exactly what Caiaphas had hoped to avoid. The testimony of Jesus' resurrection power did not fade into silence. Quite the opposite. The disciples were emboldened, and the Spirit erupted with power. The disciples ignored Caiaphas's threats, and their allegiance to Jesus intensified. Every time Caiaphas tried to put his foot down, not only did the efforts Jesus launched not stop—they multiplied.

MAKING CONNECTIONS

An important part of understanding the meaning of a Bible passage is getting a sense of its place in the broader storyline of Scripture. When we make connections between different parts of the Bible, we get a glimpse of the unity and cohesion of the Scriptures.

Caiaphas's failures should make us cringe. His example leaves us all wanting a different kind of leader: someone who would fulfill the role of priest with integrity and sacrifice.

And maybe that is the point. These archetypes in Scripture that highlight religious people who fall short of God's righteousness—perhaps they all point us to Jesus, the ultimate leader, who never fails us.

Jesus certainly proves to be a better high priest than Caiaphas. In fact, according to the book of Hebrews, he is the Ultimate High Priest.

6. **Read Hebrews 7:26–8:6 and underline anything that tells us what kind of high priest Jesus is.**

26 **For this is the kind of high priest we need: holy, innocent, undefiled, separated from sinners, and exalted above the heavens.** 27 **He doesn't need to offer sacrifices every day, as high priests do—first for their own sins, then for those of the people. He did this once for all time when he offered himself.** 28 **For the law appoints as high priests men who are weak, but the promise of the oath, which came after the law, appoints a Son, who has been perfected forever.**

8 Now the main point of what is being said is this: We have this kind of high priest, who sat down at the right hand of the throne of the Majesty in the heavens, ² a minister of the sanctuary and the true tabernacle that was set up by the Lord and not man. ³ For every high priest is appointed to offer gifts and sacrifices; therefore, it was necessary for this priest also to have something to offer. ⁴ Now if he were on earth, he wouldn't be a priest, since there are those offering the gifts prescribed by the law. ⁵ These serve as a copy and shadow of the heavenly things, as Moses was warned when he was about to complete the tabernacle. For God said, **Be careful that you make everything according to the pattern that was shown to you on the mountain.** ⁶ But Jesus has now obtained a superior ministry, and to that degree he is the mediator of a better covenant, which has been established on better promises.

HEBREWS 7:26–8:6

When religious leaders fail and cling to power, look to Jesus. Jesus is the High Priest who never fails. He won't choose his own self-interest over yours. He won't abandon the ways of God for political expediency. Jesus won't try to quiet your testimony or threaten you in order to get his way.

Jesus, the Great High Priest, has shown us what kind of leader he is. He is the kind who will go to the cross for our sins and raise us up to new life and freedom.

✦ ✦ ✦

Let's check back in on our Saints Storyline.

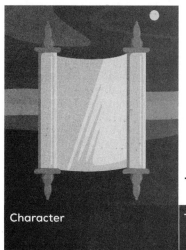

THE SAINTS STORYLINE OF SCRIPTURE

Character	They represent . . .	How did they treat Jesus?
Nicodemus (John 3, 7, 19)	religious leaders who don't accept Jesus' teaching as the way of truth.	Nicodemus didn't accept Jesus' answers.
Judas (John 6, 12, 13, 18)	religious leaders who don't stay loyal to Jesus.	Judas betrayed Jesus.
Caiaphas (John 11, 18; Acts 4)	religious leaders who oppose the work of Christ and try to preserve power by any means necessary.	Caiaphas opposed Jesus.
Peter (John 18, 21)	religious leaders who deny Jesus with their words and actions when their reputations are on the line.	Peter denied Jesus.
Paul (Acts 8; 1 Timothy 1)	religious leaders who think the end justifies the means.	Paul persecuted Jesus.

What do we learn about Jesus?	Light and Darkness Imagery
Jesus tells the truth.	Nicodemus came to Jesus at night.
Jesus is loyal.	Judas betrayed Jesus at night.
Jesus can't be stopped.	Caiaphas's courtyard had a charcoal fire.
Jesus restores us.	Peter both denied Jesus and was restored by Jesus next to a charcoal fire.
Jesus transforms us.	Paul was blinded by a bright light.

1. **What about Caiaphas's story resonates with you most?**

2. **What did you learn about God's character in this lesson?**

3. **How should these truths shape your faith community and change you?**

RESPONDING

The purpose of Bible study is to help you become more Christlike; that's why part 4 will include journaling space for your reflection on and responses to the content and a blank checklist for actionable next steps. You'll be able to process what you're learning so that you can live out the concepts and pursue Christlikeness. Part 4 will enable you to answer the questions *What truths is this passage teaching?* and *How do I apply this to my life?*

SEVERAL QUESTIONS KEPT NAGGING ME as I studied Caiaphas's story: How did he get to this point? How did he move from serving God's people to using his influence for destruction? What signs did he miss along the way that could have prevented these failures of character? And how does Caiaphas's story intersect with our own?

As I got honest with myself about the places I let power and corruption creep in, the answer to that question became a rather long list. Caiaphas's example taught me about the stronghold of denial, the blinding power of power, the corrupting nature of sin, *and* the unstoppable love of God.

But most of all, Caiaphas is a reminder that we all have influence. Our influence might not seem particularly powerful to us, not like that of a politician or business leader. But what about our influence with our closest friends, coworkers, neighbors, loved ones, or family members? What we do and say, and how we do and say it, matters. Our words and behaviors impact everyone in our orbit.

We should feel the weight of that responsibility, yes. But when we put power in its proper place, we're also invited to experience the joy that comes with the opportunity to give God glory by stewarding his power and delegating it to others.

Here are two ways you and I can use our influence for good.

1. SIDE WITH JESUS.

Caiaphas was never on Jesus' side. At every point we see him in Scripture, he was on his own side. To Caiaphas, Jesus was an enemy of the state, a disrupter of the peace, a scapegoat he was willing to have murdered, a miracle worker who needed to be silenced, evidence that needed to be buried, and a threat to his position of authority.

Part of following Jesus is choosing to abandon your "side," to join Jesus wherever he is and in whatever he is doing, and to mirror the way he accomplished his mission. When we side with Jesus, we will know it. Because he will be our most loyal friend, not an enemy. He will be our scapegoat, but willingly. He will work miracles that we will want to shout about from the rooftops. He will be our evidence for a life changed. And he will be the power in our lives, no matter our social status.

If you wonder where you stand—whether you are siding with Jesus or protecting your self-interest—look around. If you find yourself standing with people interested in worldly power and self-protection, find where Jesus is working instead. It's time to switch sides.

2. CELEBRATE RESURRECTION.

I'll never get over Lazarus. He'd been dead four days. His rotting, stinky dead body was buried in a tomb. All hope had been lost. Then Jesus wept with compassion and resurrected with power.

Undoubtedly, Lazarus's sisters, Mary and Martha, erupted with joy. They literally could not contain their faith in Christ or their devotion to him: They threw an epic dinner party for Jesus in Lazarus's honor (John 12:1-8). Mary was so overcome with thanksgiving for her brother's new life in Christ and their future in God's Kingdom that she anointed Jesus at the dinner party. You get the sense that even days after Lazarus's resurrection, everyone following Jesus was still celebrating the miracle.

You and I should be that way too. If we see broken relationships mended, trust restored, promotions attained, dreams realized, hopes revived, we should be celebrating. Because these are reasons to celebrate God at work in the lives of those we care about.

When resurrection came his way, Caiaphas missed an opportunity to celebrate. And his example should catch our attention. If we don't have the capacity to celebrate the good things God is doing in his people, we need to check our motives. Only when we recenter Christ as our model for leadership can we experience the joy that comes with resurrection.

Use this journaling space to process what you are learning.

Ask yourself how these truths impact your relationship with God and with others.

What is the Holy Spirit bringing to your mind as actionable next steps in your faith journey?

+

+

+

IDENTIFYING WITH JESUS WHEN YOUR REPUTATION IS ON THE LINE

PETER:
THE DISCIPLE WHO DENIES BEING CONNECTED TO JESUS

SCRIPTURE: JOHN 18, 21

PART 1

CONTEXT

Before you begin your study, we will start with the context of the story we are about to read together: the setting, both cultural and historical; the people involved; and where our passage fits in the larger setting of Scripture. All these things help us make sense of what we're reading. Understanding the context of a Bible story is fundamental to reading Scripture well. Getting your bearings before you read will enable you to answer the question *What am I about to read?*

SOCIAL STATUS IS a hot commodity where I live in Dallas, Texas.

Sustaining social status has everything to do with reputation and association. And how does a Dallasite maintain status? It has a lot to do with the boards you chair, the charities you sponsor, and who's standing next to you on your social platforms.

Even if you're not familiar with my city, you probably know what I'm talking about. The need to see and be seen is not just a Dallas issue. Society tells us that who we know is who we *are*. This is the reason many of us can be tempted to put our best face forward online to establish credibility and influence.

Although our society is growing more disconnected, more autonomous, and more focused on individualism, many still judge others based on the people—and the number of people—liking their social-media posts. In that regard, little has changed over time. The ways we measure status change, but we always find ways to evaluate others based on their friends and contacts.

Our culture has some similarities to the culture of the ancient world when it comes to social status. The honor-shame culture of biblical times grouped people in narrowly defined classes.[1] And it was almost impossible to break into a different level. When Jesus walked on earth, value was based on association. The rabbi you followed, the family you came from, the place you lived—all these prescribed a cultural location you'd be hard-pressed to change.

That's why following Jesus impacted a person's standing in the community. They were no longer defined by the social classes that already existed, the places their culture had carved out for them. Jesus was creating and inviting people into a *new* family, a new identity group.

But still, living fully into that new identity could be hard, and even can for us today. Association with Jesus isn't easy when social pressures start to close in.

You and I are about to explore stories that center Peter as a main character. Peter, one of the twelve disciples, had every reason to remain loyal to Jesus, his Savior:

+ Jesus healed Peter's mother-in-law (Matthew 8:14-15).
+ Peter witnessed Jesus heal Jarius's daughter (Mark 5:21-24, 35-43).
+ Peter walked on water through Jesus' power (Matthew 14:22-33).
+ Peter confessed Jesus as the Messiah (Matthew 16:13-20).
+ Peter stood next to Jesus during the Transfiguration (Matthew 17:1-8).
+ Peter heard all Jesus' sermons in the upper room before the Crucifixion (John 13–17).

But when his reputation was on the line, Peter denied association with Jesus.

Peter is an archetype for any Christian who has faith in Christ but also struggles with a gravitational pull toward playing it safe and saving face. If we're brave enough to look at ourselves in the mirror, Peter's story might sting a little. As I researched these passages, I resonated so deeply with Peter's shortcomings that I face-palmed several times.

I expect you'll be challenged by Peter's failings, as I was. But you're also going to see that when the pressures of the world cause us to turn toward safety, God isn't done with us. God redeemed Peter's story, and he can redeem each of ours.

The story of Peter shows how even a sincere disciple like Peter, fearful in the face of opposition, turned away from public confession of his discipleship. But all who know the rest of the story are encouraged that this same man will soon become a courageous preacher after being restored by Jesus and empowered by the Spirit.[2]

Pratap C. Gine and Jacob Cherian, "John," in *South Asia Bible Commentary*

Peter's storyline doesn't end with his denial of Christ. Instead, God's pursuit of Peter highlights the unyielding nature of God's power to restore. Peter's storyline doesn't finish with his ministry flakiness. The Word of God writes him a different ending: with an identity as a rock-solid foundation for the early church.

To anyone who's vacillating between being all-in for Jesus and pretending he means nothing to you, you're not alone. One of the strongest pillars of our faith cracked under pressure—yet he still found restoration and enjoyed God's favor, Christ's fellowship, and the power of the Spirit.

The opportunity before us now is to learn from Peter's pitfalls and discover how to get back up. Because in God's social economy, even his most fickle followers can become symbols of stability.

1. **PERSONAL CONTEXT: What is going on in your life right now that might impact how you understand this Bible character?**

2. **SPIRITUAL CONTEXT: If you've never studied this Bible character before, what piques your curiosity? If you've studied this character before, what impressions and insights do you recall?**

SEEING

Seeing the text is vital if we want the heart of the Scripture passage to sink in. We read slowly and intentionally through the text with the context in mind. As we practice close, thoughtful reading of Scripture, we pick up on phrases, implications, and meanings we might otherwise have missed. Part 2 includes close Scripture reading and observation questions to empower you to answer the question *What is the story saying?*

1. **Read John 18:1-27. In the margin, number each time Peter denies Jesus.**

18 After Jesus had said these things, he went out with his disciples across the Kidron Valley, where there was a garden, and he and his disciples went into it. ² Judas, who betrayed him, also knew the place, because Jesus often met there with his disciples. ³ So Judas took a company of soldiers and some officials from the chief priests and the Pharisees and came there with lanterns, torches, and weapons.

⁴ Then Jesus, knowing everything that was about to happen to him, went out and said to them, "Who is it that you're seeking?"

⁵ "Jesus of Nazareth," they answered.

"I am he," Jesus told them.

Judas, who betrayed him, was also standing with them. ⁶ When Jesus told them, "I am he," they stepped back and fell to the ground.

⁷ Then he asked them again, "Who is it that you're seeking?"

"Jesus of Nazareth," they said.

⁸ "I told you I am he," Jesus replied. "So if you're looking for me, let these men go." ⁹ This was to fulfill the words he had said: "I have not lost one of those you have given me."

¹⁰ Then Simon Peter, who had a sword, drew it, struck the high priest's servant, and cut off his right ear. (The servant's name was Malchus.)

¹¹ At that, Jesus said to Peter, "Put your sword away! Am I not to drink the cup the Father has given me?"

¹² Then the company of soldiers, the commander, and the Jewish officials arrested Jesus and tied him up. ¹³ First they led him to Annas, since he was the father-in-law of Caiaphas, who was high priest that year. ¹⁴ Caiaphas was the one who had advised the Jews that it would be better for one man to die for the people.

¹⁵ Simon Peter was following Jesus, as was another disciple. That disciple was an acquaintance of the high priest; so he went with Jesus into the high priest's courtyard. ¹⁶ But Peter remained standing outside by the door. So the other disciple, the one known to the high priest, went out and spoke to the girl who was the doorkeeper and brought Peter in.

¹⁷ Then the servant girl who was the doorkeeper said to Peter, "You aren't one of this man's disciples too, are you?"

"I am not," he said. ¹⁸ Now the servants and the officials had made a charcoal fire, because it was cold. They were standing there warming themselves, and Peter was standing with them, warming himself.

¹⁹ The high priest questioned Jesus about his disciples and about his teaching.

²⁰ "I have spoken openly to the world," Jesus answered him. "I have always taught in the synagogue and in the temple, where all the Jews gather, and I haven't spoken anything in secret. ²¹ Why do you question me? Question those who heard what I told them. Look, they know what I said."

²² When he had said these things, one of the officials standing by slapped Jesus, saying, "Is this the way you answer the high priest?"

²³ "If I have spoken wrongly," Jesus answered him, "give evidence about the wrong; but if rightly, why do you hit me?" ²⁴ Then Annas sent him bound to Caiaphas the high priest.

²⁵ Now Simon Peter was standing and warming himself. They said to him, "You aren't one of his disciples too, are you?"

He denied it and said, "I am not."

²⁶ One of the high priest's servants, a relative of the man whose ear Peter had cut off, said, "Didn't I see you with him in the garden?" ²⁷ Peter denied it again. Immediately a rooster crowed.

JOHN 18:1-27

2. **How did Peter respond when other people were turning against Jesus? (See John 18:10-11.)**

3. **Write out what Jesus says to Peter in John 18:11:**

4. What is Peter doing in John 18:15?

Peter was following Jesus. That's what he was supposed to be doing, what he had been doing for some time. But look with me at where Peter went wrong. John 18:16 says that when John followed Jesus into the high priest's courtyard, Peter remained standing outside by the door. Somewhere between the garden and the courtyard, Peter decided to stop following Jesus. He eventually made it into the courtyard, but he did so reluctantly. For the rest of the scene, Peter is not where he should be. He's not by Christ's side—he's standing apart from him.

5. Peter denies Jesus three times in this scene. Fill in the chart below to compare each denial of Christ.

	Who questioned Peter?	Write out their question.	Write out Peter's answer.
Denial #1 (John 18:17-18)			
Denial #2 (John 18:25)			
Denial #3 (John 18:26-27)			

The servant's last question clues us in to why Peter denied Christ. That question—"Didn't I see you *with him* in the garden?"—is an accusation by association. Peter denied Christ because he didn't want to be known as the guy "with Jesus." When his reputation was on the line, the great disciple Peter was reduced to denial. His loyalty faltered. His devotion wavered.

Maybe, like me, you know what this moment felt like. It came down to looking good or looking like Jesus, and we took the easy way out. Our standing in the community felt more urgent than our identification with Christ.

Denying Christ with our words or actions can be defeating. Shame and embarrassment always follow. I wonder how Peter and his friends processed this milestone moment in their faith and in their friendships.

This whole chapter, John 18, is weighty. Judas's betrayal, the arrest, Peter's denial. No wonder Jesus came undone in the garden of Gethsemane (Luke 22:44). He knew everything that was about to happen to him (John 18:4). And yet Jesus still chose to endure this agony to secure our place with him.

When his reputation was on the line, Peter couldn't find the courage to be connected to Jesus. But Jesus was going to stop at nothing to be connected to us. He put not only his reputation but also his life on the line.

6. **Look up Matthew 18:21-22 and summarize this moment in Peter and Jesus' friendship. What did Jesus teach Peter?**

7. If Peter recalled this conversation after denying Jesus, how might it have impacted Peter?

That's the good news in this sobering story. Jesus identifies with us when we want nothing to do with him. Jesus is with us always, even if we stop following him closely. No matter what we do or how far we fall, we can't exhaust Jesus' capacity to forgive. We can try to push God away, turn our backs on him, or hide altogether. But he's always right there with us.

PART 3

UNDERSTANDING

Now that we've finished a close reading of the Scriptures, we're going to spend some time on interpretation: doing our best to understand what God was saying to the original audience and what he's teaching us through the process. But to do so, we need to learn his ways and consider how God's Word would have been understood by the original audience before applying the same truths to our own lives. "Scripture interpretation" may sound a little stuffy, but understanding what God means to communicate to us in the Bible is crucial to enjoying a close relationship with Jesus. Part 3 will enable you to answer the question *What does it mean?*

PETER NEVER STOPPED LOVING JESUS. He just stopped following the One he said he'd always follow. Instead, pressure, fear, and the judgment of others made him lose track of his steps. Without Christ by his side, Peter didn't have the grit to be loyal.

Now that Jesus has ascended into heaven, you and I don't have to worry about leaving Christ's physical side the way Peter did. But that doesn't make our struggles any less challenging. Following Jesus is still hard. It just looks different.

The pressure to leave Christ's side might look like downplaying our commitment to our faith while dating so that person doesn't judge us for being too religious. It could look like hiding the fact that we are Christ followers at work so that we don't rock the boat. Any scenario in our lives where we can identify with

Christ or make our association with him clear but choose not to—that's similar to Peter's denial of Christ.

1. In your own life, have you ever noticed a reluctance to acknowledge your relationship with Christ? If so, what motivated you? What fears impacted your decision? If you acted on your reluctance in some way, how did you feel afterward?

2. How do you think Peter's denial of Christ impacted how he viewed himself?

3. How do you think Peter's denial of Christ impacted his relationship with the other disciples?

We know from other places in the Gospels that the disciples got into arguments with one another, as friends do. I wonder if Peter's denial of Christ fractured the disciples' trust of each other like never before.

MAKING CONNECTIONS

An important part of understanding the meaning of a Bible passage is getting a sense of its place in the broader storyline of Scripture. When we make connections between different parts of the Bible, we get a glimpse of the unity and cohesion of the Scriptures.

John concludes his Gospel account of Jesus' life, death, and resurrection by narrating a final, profound moment: The resurrected Jesus seeks out Peter, the man who denied him, and restores him to leadership.

This ending to John's historical biography of Jesus gives us further concrete evidence that we can and should believe that Jesus is the Messiah. But I don't believe that this is the story's only purpose in the Scriptures. John may have included this story in his Gospel also because it was important to him personally.

John had been in business with Peter long before they ever encountered Christ. In the years following Jesus' invitation to "fish for men" (Luke 5:10, NLV), John and Peter had shared countless meals together and linked arms in ministry to heal and preach during Christ's life on earth. Even more, these two men were part of Jesus' inner circle, set apart from the other disciples to enjoy intimacy with Christ and special moments like the Transfiguration (Matthew 17:1-8). So when Peter denied Christ, he didn't just deny his Savior—he turned his back on his closest friends. His new family in Christ.

Jesus wasn't the only one seeking resolution to Peter's denial. John needed resolution too. When we are in community with other Christians, the redemption of our friends can be a powerful part of our personal stories. In my own life, watching others accept the consequences of their sin and be restored to leadership after repentance and healing has strengthened my faith in Christ.

4. Read John 21:1-19. Each time Jesus restores Peter to leadership with a question, number the question in the margin.

21 After this, Jesus revealed himself again to his disciples by the Sea of Tiberias. He revealed himself in this way:

² Simon Peter, Thomas (called "Twin"), Nathanael from Cana of Galilee, Zebedee's sons, and two others of his disciples were together.

³ "I'm going fishing," Simon Peter said to them.

"We're coming with you," they told him. They went out and got into the boat, but that night they caught nothing.

⁴ When daybreak came, Jesus stood on the shore, but the disciples did not know it was Jesus. ⁵ "Friends," Jesus called to them, "you don't have any fish, do you?"

"No," they answered.

⁶ "Cast the net on the right side of the boat," he told them, "and you'll find some." So they did, and they were unable to haul it in because of the large number of fish. ⁷ The disciple, the one Jesus loved, said to Peter, "It is the Lord!"

When Simon Peter heard that it was the Lord, he tied his outer clothing around him (for he had taken it off) and plunged into the sea. ⁸ Since they were not far from land (about a hundred yards away), the other disciples came in the boat, dragging the net full of fish.

⁹ When they got out on land, they saw a charcoal fire there, with fish lying on it, and bread. ¹⁰ "Bring some of the fish you've just caught," Jesus told them. ¹¹ So Simon Peter climbed up and hauled the net ashore, full of large fish—153 of them. Even though there were so many, the net was not torn.

¹² "Come and have breakfast," Jesus told them. None of the disciples dared ask him, "Who are you?" because they knew it was the Lord. ¹³ Jesus came, took the bread, and gave it to them. He did the same with the fish. ¹⁴ This was now the third time Jesus appeared to the disciples after he was raised from the dead.

¹⁵ When they had eaten breakfast, Jesus asked Simon Peter, "Simon, son of John, do you love me more than these?"

"Yes, Lord," he said to him, "you know that I love you."

"Feed my lambs," he told him. ¹⁶ A second time he asked him, "Simon, son of John, do you love me?"

"Yes, Lord," he said to him, "you know that I love you."

"Shepherd my sheep," he told him.

¹⁷ He asked him the third time, "Simon, son of John, do you love me?"

Peter was grieved that he asked him the third time, "Do you love me?" He said, "Lord, you know everything; you know that I love you."

"Feed my sheep," Jesus said. ¹⁸ "Truly I tell you, when you were younger, you would tie your belt and walk wherever you wanted. But when you grow old, you will stretch out your hands and someone else will tie you and carry you where you don't want to go." ¹⁹ He said this to indicate by what kind of death Peter would glorify God. After saying this, he told him, "Follow me."

JOHN 21:1-19

5. **When Peter recognized Jesus, what did he do next? How was Peter's reaction different from the reactions of the other disciples in the boat?**

Peter could not wait to be near Jesus, to stand close by him, to follow him. Peter had experienced the devastation of choosing to step away from Jesus, the complete agony of that loss, and he wasn't going to miss another minute. And for the disciples who watched Peter swim to shore—was Peter's return to his Savior's side the restoration they all needed to experience?

The rest of the story has a tender place in my heart. If you need to be reminded of God's compassion, his unfailing love, his loyal protection, and his willingness to forgive, stick with Peter's story a little longer.

6. Jesus restores Peter to leadership three times in this scene. Fill in the chart below to compare each part of Jesus' conversation with Peter.

	What was Jesus' question to Peter?	Write out Peter's answer.	Write out Jesus' command to Peter.
Restoration #1 (John 21:15)			
Restoration #2 (John 21:16)			
Restoration #3 (John 21:17)			

Don't miss it: Jesus' threefold repetition is a sacred echo of Peter's threefold denial. Jesus saw Peter fully, the tangled web of fear and failure and longing to love. Jesus never stopped loving Peter, and Peter never stopped loving Jesus. As revolutionary as it may be, Peter's storyline does not end with a lifetime of shame and failure to launch. Redemption is the storyline.

Peter's friends heard every word of this conversation. They were witnesses to Jesus' loyal love. Jesus didn't restore just his relationship with Peter or Peter's leadership calling. Jesus had this conversation in front of the other disciples to restore Peter's relationship with his friends. It doesn't surprise me that later in Peter's story, John is often right beside him, leading the church against opposition. Together, they knew the power of redemption.

Let's check back in on our Saints Storyline.

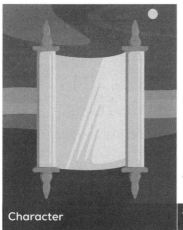

THE SAINTS STORYLINE OF SCRIPTURE

Character	They represent . . .	How did they treat Jesus?
Nicodemus (John 3, 7, 19)	religious leaders who don't accept Jesus' teaching as the way of truth.	Nicodemus didn't accept Jesus' answers.
Judas (John 6, 12, 13, 18)	religious leaders who don't stay loyal to Jesus.	Judas betrayed Jesus.
Caiaphas (John 11, 18; Acts 4)	religious leaders who oppose the work of Christ and try to preserve power by any means necessary.	Caiaphas opposed Jesus.
Peter (John 18, 21)	religious leaders who deny Jesus with their words and actions when their reputations are on the line.	Peter denied Jesus.
Paul (Acts 8; 1 Timothy 1)	religious leaders who think the end justifies the means.	Paul persecuted Jesus.

What do we learn about Jesus?	Light and Darkness Imagery
Jesus tells the truth.	Nicodemus came to Jesus at night.
Jesus is loyal.	Judas betrayed Jesus at night.
Jesus can't be stopped.	Caiaphas's courtyard had a charcoal fire.
Jesus restores us.	Peter both denied Jesus and was restored by Jesus next to a charcoal fire.
Jesus transforms us.	Paul was blinded by a bright light.

1. What about Peter's story resonates with you most?

2. What did you learn about God's character in this lesson?

3. How should these truths shape your faith community and change you?

RESPONDING

The purpose of Bible study is to help you become more Christlike; that's why part 4 will include journaling space for your reflection on and responses to the content and a blank checklist for actionable next steps. You'll be able to process what you're learning so that you can live out the concepts and pursue Christlikeness. Part 4 will enable you to answer the questions *What truths is this passage teaching?* and *How do I apply this to my life?*

I HAD NO IDEA MY SON, CALEB, had been paying attention to church sermons until Good Friday 2020. He and I were perched on the patio in our backyard, soaking up the sun, when he asked me if his dad would be preaching out of Romans 6 for that evening's church service. My jaw practically touched the ground.

Caleb explained that he'd been following along in services and noticed that Aaron, who is the lead pastor at our church, was going chapter by chapter through the book of Romans. Logically, he thought, we'd be going through the next chapter of Romans at the next service—Good Friday.

My eyes must have blinked a hundred times as I tried to rally for this moment. "No," I told Caleb. "Your dad isn't preaching out of Romans tonight. He's going to teach through John 21." Without skipping a beat, Caleb asked if we could please read John 21 together so he would be up to speed.

Caleb finished reading John 21 out loud, closed his Bible, and buried his head in both his hands. It's a moment I'll never forget. Jesus' conversation with Peter touched a tender place in Caleb. When I questioned him about how he was processing the passage, he said, "Jesus is *awesome*."

What was it that Caleb considered awesome about Jesus? "Jesus could have chosen new friends. But he wanted Peter."

Out of the mouth of babes, y'all.

Caleb was all ears during the Good Friday worship service. Peter's restoration taught Caleb that his Savior Jesus would be his friend no matter what.

Maybe you need to hear that today: Jesus is your friend no matter what. If Peter's failings look like child's play compared to your own, remember this. Jesus Christ is the same yesterday, today, and forever (Hebrews 13:8). His loyalty does not change based on your behavior. Jesus loves you still. You have a friend in Jesus always.

Peter went on to become a pillar of the early church movement (Galatians 1:18). He was the first leader of the church in Jerusalem, the first missionary to the Gentiles (Acts 10), and a bold preacher of the gospel (Acts 2–4).

How? How does someone like Peter move past his past? Let's consider two thoughts.

1. EVEN WHEN I FALL AWAY, JESUS RESTORES ME.

If you feel distant from close fellowship with Jesus, don't be afraid. Don't get overwhelmed or discouraged. See where Jesus is at work, get close to the action, and enjoy returning to your place by his side. He's reserved a place for you, even when you feel like you're standing outside his grace. In the same way Jesus called out to Peter, Jesus is calling to you: *Friend!* In Peter's story, Jesus gathered Peter and some of the other disciples near a fire to share breakfast. That's the Savior you follow. He's the One who extends an invitation to you so that you can enjoy his friendship again.

> The Christian life does not consist in achieving great things for God but in allowing Jesus to use our inadequacy and failure to rehabilitate us to a life experienced as grace and love and obedience.[4]
>
> Eugene H. Peterson,
> *As Kingfishers Catch Fire*

No matter how far you feel you've fallen or walked away from Christ, restoration is possible. Confess your sins to God and enjoy the redemption he extends to you. He is so gracious. He can't wait to welcome you back into his presence.

2. EVEN WHEN I DISQUALIFY MYSELF, JESUS CAN REINSTATE ME.

Jesus belabored his point with Peter—emphasizing three times how committed Peter would need to be going forward in ministry. Peter was "grieved" that Jesus had to ask him so many times if he loved him (John 21:17). Jesus knew better than anyone that Peter's love had never been in question. It was his willingness to be identified and associated with Jesus that needed to be interrogated.

If you're grieving how royally you've disqualified yourself, you're not alone in that sadness. It is healthy to lament disloyalty to Jesus. A needed rite of passage, even. Once you've addressed your sin through repentance, you need someone to challenge your devotion to God so that you are prepared for the inevitable tests of your faith in the future. Being in service to God requires fidelity to Jesus alone. But take heart. If you've disqualified yourself in the past, Peter proves that Jesus can restore you.

Use this journaling space to process what you are learning.

Ask yourself how these truths impact your relationship with God and with others.

What is the Holy Spirit bringing to your mind as actionable next steps in your faith journey?

+

+

+

REGAINING CLARITY WHEN YOU'RE BLINDED BY PASSION

PAUL:
THE PHARISEE WHO PERSECUTES CHRISTIANS

SCRIPTURE: ACTS 8; 1 TIMOTHY 1

PART 1

CONTEXT

Before you begin your study, we will start with the context of the story we are about to read together: the setting, both cultural and historical; the people involved; and where our passage fits in the larger setting of Scripture. All these things help us make sense of what we're reading. Understanding the context of a Bible story is fundamental to reading Scripture well. Getting your bearings before you read will enable you to answer the question *What am I about to read?*

IF YOU ASK MY NINE-YEAR-OLD SON why he likes the book of Acts, he'll tell you it's because a lot of people go to jail. He's not wrong.

+ Peter and John are arrested for proclaiming the resurrection of the dead through Jesus (Acts 4:1-22).
+ The apostles are arrested for performing signs and wonders in Jesus' name (Acts 5:12-42).
+ After James is executed by King Herod, Peter goes back to jail and stays there until the angel of the Lord busts him out (Acts 12:1-19).
+ Paul and Silas are thrown in prison for casting a demon out of a slave girl in Philippi (Acts 16:16-40).

The book of Acts details the growth of the early church and the inevitable opposition they faced for suggesting that Jesus, not Caesar, was Lord. And while jail time is a common theme in the book of Acts, going to jail was one of the least severe forms of resistance the disciples faced. Threats of physical violence and even death were ever present.

One of the most zealous persecutors of the early church was a man named Saul, whom we know as Paul throughout most of the rest of the New Testament. Paul was one of the Pharisees, the elite religious group of Jewish men best known for their careful interpretations of the law of Moses.

Unfortunately, the word *Pharisee* is often used today as a pejorative description of someone who is legalistic, heartless, and mean. But the historical records paint a different picture of the Pharisees and their objectives. Contemporary perspectives didn't see the Pharisees as motivated by hate or greed. In fact, the opposite was true.

As we learned earlier, the Pharisees were regarded as some of the most gracious, most lenient interpreters of the law. Pharisees existed to help the Jewish working class participate in Temple life. They wanted to see more people enjoy God's fellowship through Temple worship and to ensure that all—not just the wealthy—could apply the Torah to their lives. The Pharisees cared so deeply for the common people that they expanded the applications of the law in ways that were generous and inclusive.

In resorting to violence, Paul was in the minority of Pharisees. He represents not all Pharisees and all Jews but rather those in a group who are willing to use the end to justify the means.

The aim of Pharisaism can be described as sanctification: the whole nation (not just the priests) stands under the command to be holy. . . . The way to holiness is a life according to the Torah. Therefore, *all* Israel should know the Law and be encouraged to keep it.[1]

Roland Deines, "Pharisees," in *The Eerdmans Dictionary of Early Judaism*

Most Pharisees in the New Testament were not convinced that Jesus was the Messiah, so they were disturbed when they saw well-intentioned Jews following Jesus. Paul took this a step further. Convinced that faith in Jesus was leading people astray—and being singularly devoted to righteous living and finding ways to help others live righteously—Paul was outraged at what Christians were doing. What began as vigilance to follow the law of God, to honor God with his whole life, turned into spiritual blindness with destructive consequences.

Paul's obsession with rooting out the "lie" that Jesus was Lord turned him into a religious terrorist blinded by passion. He was so distracted by a potential threat to the truth, he almost missed Messiah Jesus—the Way, the Truth, and the Life (John 14:6).

> Their [Pharisaic] aim was to shape the Torah tradition so that it could be practiced by as many people as possible during their daily routine.[2]
>
> Roland Deines, "Pharisees," in *The Eerdmans Dictionary of Early Judaism*

Tragically, Paul hurt Christians in his crusade—and he hurt himself, too. Yes, he was putting others in jail. But he'd also bound himself in self-righteousness. He'd put himself in a prison of his own making. Isn't that how life goes? Our fervent priorities sometimes morph into destructive patterns that keep us trapped in our own pain and out of alignment with God's ways.

What we're about to see is Paul's "arresting encounter" with the risen Jesus.[3] Paul had been ravaging the church and dragging Christian men and women to jail for their faith in Christ. But everything changed when he met Jesus on the road to Damascus.

We're going to read about the scales falling off Paul's eyes so that he could see again, physically and spiritually. Paul shows us how to be captivated by Jesus and regain a vision for God's Kingdom. A reality where violence has no place. A reality where we are safe to worship God and to see clearly his gracious and loving ways.

Caleb Armstrong makes a good point about the book of Acts: A lot of people do go to jail. But a lot of people also get set free. And Paul is one of them. If you need more freedom in your life, this final lesson is for you.

In the same way Paul was set free from his blinding passions, we, too, can experience liberation from spiritual blindness. Let's be done with the jails and prisons of our own making. Instead, let's enjoy the liberties that Christ's life, death, and resurrection have secured for us all. May the arresting power of God give us all a vision of our freedom in Christ.

1. **PERSONAL CONTEXT: What is going on in your life right now that might impact how you understand this Bible character?**

2. **SPIRITUAL CONTEXT: If you've never studied this Bible character before, what piques your curiosity? If you've studied this character before, what impressions and insights do you recall?**

SEEING

Seeing the text is vital if we want the heart of the Scripture passage to sink in. We read slowly and intentionally through the text with the context in mind. As we practice close, thoughtful reading of Scripture, we pick up on phrases, implications, and meanings we might otherwise have missed. Part 2 includes close Scripture reading and observation questions to empower you to answer the question *What is the story saying?*

1. **Read Acts 9:1-22 and underline everything Jesus says in the story.**

9 Now Saul was still breathing threats and murder against the disciples of the Lord. He went to the high priest ² and requested letters from him to the synagogues in Damascus, so that if he found any men or women who belonged to the Way, he might bring them as prisoners to Jerusalem. ³ As he traveled and was nearing Damascus, a light from heaven suddenly flashed around him. ⁴ Falling to the ground, he heard a voice saying to him, "Saul, Saul, why are you persecuting me?"

⁵ "Who are you, Lord?" Saul said.

"I am Jesus, the one you are persecuting," he replied. ⁶ "But get up and go into the city, and you will be told what you must do."

[7] The men who were traveling with him stood speechless, hearing the sound but seeing no one. [8] Saul got up from the ground, and though his eyes were open, he could see nothing. So they took him by the hand and led him into Damascus. [9] He was unable to see for three days and did not eat or drink.

[10] There was a disciple in Damascus named Ananias, and the Lord said to him in a vision, "Ananias."

"Here I am, Lord," he replied.

[11] "Get up and go to the street called Straight," the Lord said to him, "to the house of Judas, and ask for a man from Tarsus named Saul, since he is praying there. [12] In a vision he has seen a man named Ananias coming in and placing his hands on him so that he may regain his sight."

[13] "Lord," Ananias answered, "I have heard from many people about this man, how much harm he has done to your saints in Jerusalem. [14] And he has authority here from the chief priests to arrest all who call on your name."

[15] But the Lord said to him, "Go, for this man is my chosen instrument to take my name to Gentiles, kings, and Israelites. [16] I will show him how much he must suffer for my name."

[17] Ananias went and entered the house. He placed his hands on him and said, "Brother Saul, the Lord Jesus, who appeared to you on the road you were traveling, has sent me so that you may regain your sight and be filled with the Holy Spirit."

Saul, then, was not just a hothead with a fiery brand of theology. He was a violent zealot of the most extreme kind, believing that God was sponsoring his violence and that he was therefore justified in seeking to destroy anyone who he thought endangered Israel's national purity and hence Israel's future hope.[4]

N. T. Wright and Michael F. Bird, *The New Testament in Its World*

¹⁸ At once something like scales fell from his eyes, and he regained his sight. Then he got up and was baptized. ¹⁹ And after taking some food, he regained his strength.

Saul was with the disciples in Damascus for some time. ²⁰ Immediately he began proclaiming Jesus in the synagogues: "He is the Son of God."

²¹ All who heard him were astounded and said, "Isn't this the man in Jerusalem who was causing havoc for those who called on this name and came here for the purpose of taking them as prisoners to the chief priests?"

²² But Saul grew stronger and kept confounding the Jews who lived in Damascus by proving that Jesus is the Messiah.

ACTS 9:1-22

2. **List all the ways Paul was persecuting the church:**

✦

✦

✦

✦

Persecuting the Christians in Jerusalem was only the beginning for Saul. He was willing to travel to Damascus to terrorize the Christians there, too. One of the literary themes in the book of Acts is the progression of the gospel from Jerusalem through Samaria and eventually to the ends of the earth. With this story in Acts 9, Luke, the author of the book of Acts, seems to be signaling to his readers who are familiar with this theme of expansion: Just as the gospel was spreading, so was the opposition to Christ and his followers. The truth was moving beyond Jerusalem, and so were persecutors like Paul.

3. Describe or draw what the men traveling with Paul had to do to get him into the city of Damascus after his encounter with Christ (Acts 9:8).

Paul had planned to lead Christians out of Damascus with their hands chained. Now he was the one who needed the hands of others to lead him into the city.

He is required to rely on others for existence, and even to rely on Ananias, one he would have led away in chains, for sight.[5]

Margaret Aymer, "Acts of the Apostles," in *Women's Bible Commentary*

4. Paul prayed for three days (Acts 9:9-11). Write out what you imagine he prayed.

5. How did God prepare Paul to meet Ananias? (See Acts 9:12.)

☐ with a document
☐ with a vision

God's storytelling is unmatched. Paul was blinded by religious zeal and then blinded by Jesus' presence. But God opens eyes. Paul couldn't see, but God gave him a vision of his future.

This point in Paul's story brought me great comfort as I considered all the ways I may be unaware of what God is doing in my life. When my eyes fail me, when my perspective is darkened by my sin, I can be confident of this: Jesus has the power to illuminate my understanding and give me a vision of the future. Nothing can keep Jesus from showing each of us the way of truth.

6. **List at least two reasons Ananias was hesitant to follow the Lord's instructions in Acts 9:13-14.**

Much like Paul at this point in the story, Ananias could not see clearly how God's plan would unfold. Logically, a Christian like Ananias should have felt terrified to approach the most zealous religious terrorist of the day. Paul's reputation, the chief priests' endorsement of his persecution, and the testimony of other Christians were reasons enough for Ananias to reject God's plan. But Ananias chose to obey God over fearing Paul.

7. **In Acts 9:15-16, the Lord tells Ananias that Paul will suffer for the name of Christ. After reading the passage, list the sufferings Paul ended up enduring for his faith in Jesus. Use Paul's own words from 2 Corinthians 11:24-28.**

24 Five times I received the forty lashes minus one from the Jews. 25 Three times I was beaten with rods. Once I received a stoning. Three times I was shipwrecked. I have spent a night and a day in the open sea. 26 On

frequent journeys, I faced dangers from rivers, dangers from robbers, dangers from my own people, dangers from Gentiles, dangers in the city, dangers in the wilderness, dangers at sea, and dangers among false brothers; ²⁷ toil and hardship, many sleepless nights, hunger and thirst, often without food, cold, and without clothing. ²⁸ Not to mention other things, there is the daily pressure on me: my concern for all the churches.

2 CORINTHIANS 11:24-28

The sufferings Paul endured for Christ:

+

+

+

+

+

+

+

+

+

+

8. How did Ananias address Paul the first time they met? (See Acts 9:17.)

Between the time Ananias received a vision from the Lord and the moment he met Paul in person, Ananias changed his perspective. No longer was Paul his enemy. Paul was Ananias's new brother in Christ. He'd gone from persecutor to part of the family.

What a beautiful hope we all have in Christ. Even if our lives before Christ were filled with antagonism, our past behavior doesn't have to define our current relationships. In Christ, our siblingship is based on grace. You've received it. I've received it. And together, we share a connection that cannot be broken.

Yes, Paul still faced consequences for his persecution of God's people. He still had to build trust with the disciples and the rest of the church. But, thank God, Paul's consequences didn't keep him from connection with the other disciples of Christ.

This is the family of God and the way of Jesus: uncommon kindness and laying down fear to welcome even our enemies—or to find ourselves welcomed, despite our pasts.

PART 3

UNDERSTANDING

Now that we've finished a close reading of the Scriptures, we're going to spend some time on interpretation: doing our best to understand what God was saying to the original audience and what he's teaching us through the process. But to do so, we need to learn his ways and consider how God's Word would have been understood by the original audience before applying the same truths to our own lives. "Scripture interpretation" may sound a little stuffy, but understanding what God means to communicate to us in the Bible is crucial to enjoying a close relationship with Jesus. Part 3 will enable you to answer the question *What does it mean?*

I AM ONE OF THE MILLIONS OF FANS of the original *Fixer Upper*, the TV series showcasing Joanna and Chip Gaines's talent for remodeling homes. I was a sucker for the "before" and "after" pictures and the big reveal at the end of each episode. Even though I don't have the vision to remodel or redesign my own home, watching the process of change in someone else's kept me engaged. I've found the same to be true about the apostle Paul's transformation story.

Sometimes I struggle to see where God is at work in my life and to believe that he is changing me from the inside out. But then I am reminded of stories like Paul's, where we get to see some of the steps along the way, a picture of the before and after of God's radical transformation. And in one of his letters in the New Testament, Paul describes that before and after with simple and striking words.

1. **Read 1 Timothy 1:12-17 and describe Paul's before and after.**

    ¹² I give thanks to Christ Jesus our Lord who has strengthened me, because he considered me faithful, appointing me to the ministry—¹³ even though I was formerly a blasphemer, a persecutor, and an arrogant man. But I received mercy because I acted out of ignorance in unbelief, ¹⁴ and the grace of our Lord overflowed, along with the faith and love that are in Christ Jesus. ¹⁵ This saying is trustworthy and deserving of full acceptance: "Christ Jesus came into the world to save sinners"—and I am the worst of them. ¹⁶ But I received mercy for this reason, so that in me, the worst of them, Christ Jesus might demonstrate his extraordinary patience as an example to those who would believe in him for eternal life. ¹⁷ Now to the King eternal, immortal, invisible, the only God, be honor and glory forever and ever. Amen.

    1 TIMOTHY 1:12-17

Paul's Before	Paul's After

2. **Jesus could have used anything to arrest Paul's attention. Why do you think he used blindness?**

At least one of the reasons God may have chosen to afflict Paul with physical blindness was to reflect his spiritual reality: Paul was already blind, at least spiritually. Paul couldn't see past his own passions. Past his unflinching religious practice. Paul wanted to make a name for himself as *the* most zealous of God's followers, and that drive prevented him from seeing clearly: His behavior was hurting God's people and opposing the mission of the very God he claimed to serve.

It's possible that Paul's spiritual blindness had formed through fear—fear that people were going astray, fear that God's Temple would be defiled, fear that people were following a false gospel. Whatever scaled Paul's physical eyes on the road to Damascus symbolized the scales that covered his ability to discern right from wrong.

3. **When Paul regained his sight, everything looked different. Describe how Paul's perspective would have shifted on these topics:**

    + his former enemies:
    + his faith practice:
    + his life's purpose:

Paul is one of many people in Scripture who experienced this kind of radical call to follow God. God is ready to use whatever he needs to get our attention.

MAKING CONNECTIONS

An important part of understanding the meaning of a Bible passage is getting a sense of its place in the broader storyline of Scripture. When we make connections between different parts of the Bible, we get a glimpse of the unity and cohesion of the Scriptures.

My attention span is so short these days, I find it hard to focus. Which, of course, impacts my capacity to focus on my relationship with God. Sometimes I purpose to pray and end up stressing about my to-do list. I set aside time to get in the Word and end up scrolling social-media apps for one-minute videos that add no

The appearance of Jesus to Saul is described in the same manner as theophanies in the OT. The shining light is a familiar feature in the OT and elsewhere (Exod. 19:16; 2 Sam. 22:13-15; Ezek. 1:13-14; Dan. 10:6), as is a heavenly voice (Exod. 3:1-6; Isa. 6:8).[6]

I. Howard Marshall, "Acts," in *Commentary on the New Testament Use of the Old Testament*

value to my life. That's why I find God's revelations to some of the key leaders in our faith history so encouraging. When God needs to get our attention, he will. I, for one, count on his willingness to intercept us onour paths.

Paul was opposing the purposes of God, and Jesus stopped him in his tracks on the road. In Exodus 3, Moses was avoiding the purposes of God, and God stopped him in his tracks in the desert. In both cases, God's call pierced through the darkness of their sin, disorientation, and lack of understanding with a bright light.

4. Read Exodus 3:1-4 and underline what God says to Moses.

3 Meanwhile, Moses was shepherding the flock of his father-in-law Jethro, the priest of Midian. He led the flock to the far side of the wilderness and came to Horeb, the mountain of God. [2] Then the angel of the LORD appeared to him in a flame of fire within a bush. As Moses looked, he saw that the bush was on fire but was not consumed. [3] So Moses thought, "I must go over and look at this remarkable sight. Why isn't the bush burning up?"

[4] When the LORD saw that he had gone over to look, God called out to him from the bush, "Moses, Moses!"

"Here I am," he answered.

EXODUS 3:1-4

5. List any connections between Paul's call to ministry in Acts 9 and Moses' call to ministry in Exodus 3.

	Moses (Exodus 3)	Paul (Acts 9)
What were they doing before God interrupted their plans?		
How did God appear to them?		
How did they respond?		
How did God identify himself?		

If you feel as though you are in darkness, remain hopeful. Your God is true light of light. If you feel trapped in darkness, he has the power to turn on the lights.

✜ ✜ ✜

Let's check back in on our Saints Storyline.

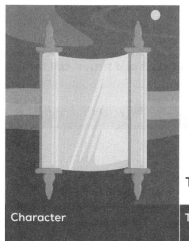

THE SAINTS STORYLINE OF SCRIPTURE

Character	They represent . . .	How did they treat Jesus?
Nicodemus (John 3, 7, 19)	religious leaders who don't accept Jesus' teaching as the way of truth.	Nicodemus didn't accept Jesus' answers.
Judas (John 6, 12, 13, 18)	religious leaders who don't stay loyal to Jesus.	Judas betrayed Jesus.
Caiaphas (John 11, 18; Acts 4)	religious leaders who oppose the work of Christ and try to preserve power by any means necessary.	Caiaphas opposed Jesus.
Peter (John 18, 21)	religious leaders who deny Jesus with their words and actions when their reputations are on the line.	Peter denied Jesus.
Paul (Acts 8; 1 Timothy 1)	religious leaders who think the end justifies the means.	Paul persecuted Jesus.

What do we learn about Jesus?	Light and Darkness Imagery
Jesus tells the truth.	Nicodemus came to Jesus at night.
Jesus is loyal.	Judas betrayed Jesus at night.
Jesus can't be stopped.	Caiaphas's courtyard had a charcoal fire.
Jesus restores us.	Peter both denied Jesus and was restored by Jesus next to a charcoal fire.
Jesus transforms us.	Paul was blinded by a bright light.

1. What about Paul's story resonates with you most?

2. What did you learn about God's character in this lesson?

3. How should these truths shape your faith community and change you?

RESPONDING

The purpose of Bible study is to help you become more Christlike; that's why part 4 will include journaling space for your reflection on and responses to the content and a blank checklist for actionable next steps. You'll be able to process what you're learning so that you can live out the concepts and pursue Christlikeness. Part 4 will enable you to answer the questions *What truths is this passage teaching?* and *How do I apply this to my life?*

GOD TRANSFORMED PAUL from persecuting believers to proclaiming the gospel. From making prisoners to setting people free. From being spiritually blind to seeing Jesus clearly as the Son of God. From arresting and condemning God's people to being arrested by God's grace. From being an enemy to being a brother.

And God can do the same for you and for me.

If judgmentalism, pride, unforgiveness, or zealous passion is a prison around you—know that God bought your freedom with the precious blood of Christ. You are free.

If you need to start again—God can do that for you. You're free.

And in the same way God called Paul to be a "chosen instrument" (Acts 9:15), God calls you: Share your freedom with others.

Let's not stay stuck in the prisons of our own making. Let's not put bars around our hearts for the sake of religion. Let's not allow our pasts to hold us back from moving forward in our calling to share God's freedom with others.

Two points in Paul's story struck me with conviction. I pray they resonate with you, too.

1. A ZEAL FOR RIGHTEOUSNESS CAN BLIND US TO THE TRUTH.

Stephen's stoning in Acts 7 should have been a wake-up call for Paul. As a violent mob did the long, heavy work of lifting and casting stones to bludgeon Stephen to death, each person made a pit stop at Paul's feet. Before hurling their condemnation on Stephen for preaching the truth of the gospel, Stephen's murderers left their garments with Paul—a sign of his approval, his complicity in this evil. One would hope, for Paul's sake and our own, that the goriness of Stephen's death would have so affected Paul, so shocked and horrified him, that he would have stepped back and realized what he had become, how far he'd moved from what the Pharisees were best known for. Instead, Stephen's death appears to have been a tipping point for Paul, the persecutor. Acts 8:1 says, "Saul agreed with putting [Stephen] to death." Paul, the great Pharisee, the great expositor of God's law, agreed more with Stephen's murder than with God's clear instruction to love God and love others.

> It was on the road to Damascus that Saul experienced a vivid and arresting encounter with the risen lord Jesus that threw his social and theological worlds into a cataclysmic upheaval.[7]
>
> N. T. Wright and Michael F. Bird, *The New Testament in Its World*

We cannot miss this: No matter how much we disagree with someone's religious practices or personal beliefs, resorting to violence is not the way of Christ. Sometimes a zeal for rightness can blind us to the truth: that God is the only Righteous One, and he is love.

2. GOD GIVES SIGHT TO THE BLIND.

God might have to send you a flashing light from heaven to get your attention, but he won't let you stay blind. God might need to interrupt your plan to get your attention, but he won't let you continue down the wrong path. You might even have to experience some form of helplessness, like Paul did, if that's what it takes for you to finally stop and assess whether your life reflects Christ.

The good news is that God will see to it that you and I have opportunities to pause, reflect, repent, and be restored. What grace. This is what we learn from Paul's story: God has the power to turn self-righteousness into self-sacrificing love. What he did for Paul, he can and will do for us. God gives sight to the blind—and I, for one, could not be more exuberantly grateful.

Use this journaling space to process what you are learning.

Ask yourself how these truths impact your relationship with God and with others.

What is the Holy Spirit bringing to your mind as actionable next steps in your faith journey?

+

+

+

As You Go

YOU DID IT. You studied five "saints" in the Bible—people who were dedicated to following God and yet acted sinfully: Nicodemus, Judas, Caiaphas, Peter, and Paul.

+ Nicodemus represents a spiritually curious religious leader resistant to Jesus' truth.
+ Judas was an apostate apostle.
+ Caiaphas represents a spiritual leader scared to lose his power.
+ Peter represents a fallen leader restored to ministry through repentance.
+ Paul represents a dogmatic religious leader freed into grace.

Notice with me what key elements Nicodemus, Judas, Caiaphas, Peter, and Paul share in the storyline of Scripture:

+ a calling to follow God;
+ an affinity for God's Word;
+ close relationship(s) with Jesus and/or Christians;

+ a defining moment or season in their life when they sinned or failed; and

+ an opportunity to repent, which could lead to restoration. Some chose to accept Jesus' forgiveness, and others did not.

All these things are likely true for you, too. They are for me. The saints storyline should grieve us, yes, but it should also give us hope: No matter how far the wandering, no matter how significant the fall, God's grace is always available. His grace breaks through when religious leaders fail us, meeting us in our discouragement and distrust. His grace breaks through when we fail, finding us in our brokenness and blindness.

Wherever you are, whatever you're facing, he loves you. And that is always, always the story he's ready to write.

Sometimes it feels like the headlines about Christian leaders and Christ followers are all about people like Nicodemus, Judas, Caiaphas, Peter, and Paul. But God is not invested in saving face; he's interested in restoration. And restoration doesn't happen without bringing the darkness into the light. The Bible does not shy away from exposing evil, even if that means lessening the credibility of characters we thought we could trust. God chose to include stories about unrighteous saints, and in doing so, he revealed the potential pitfalls of religious institutions and the unbecoming behavior of the God followers who lead them.

But thanks be to God: Religion and hypocrisy didn't stand in the way of Christ's sinless life, sacrificial death, and miraculous resurrection. And moral failures and corrupt institutions don't stand in the way of us enjoying a relationship with Jesus either. They never defined our relationship with God anyway.

Yes, it's painful when leaders fail us. Yes, this is not how it should be. But the failures of religious leaders don't get to define us. They don't get to set the terms of our joy-filled, Christ-focused faith. Only God gets to do that, and he's already written that story.

PS: I've loved this time with you, and I hope you join me again for another journey in the **Storyline Bible Studies**.

THE SAINTS STORYLINE OF SCRIPTURE

Character	They represent . . .	How did they treat Jesus?
Nicodemus (John 3, 7, 19)	religious leaders who don't accept Jesus' teaching as the way of truth.	Nicodemus didn't accept Jesus' answers.
Judas (John 6, 12, 13, 18)	religious leaders who don't stay loyal to Jesus.	Judas betrayed Jesus.
Caiaphas (John 11, 18; Acts 4)	religious leaders who oppose the work of Christ and try to preserve power by any means necessary.	Caiaphas opposed Jesus.
Peter (John 18, 21)	religious leaders who deny Jesus with their words and actions when their reputations are on the line.	Peter denied Jesus.
Paul (Acts 8; 1 Timothy 1)	religious leaders who think the end justifies the means.	Paul persecuted Jesus.

What do we learn about Jesus?	Light and Darkness Imagery
Jesus tells the truth.	Nicodemus came to Jesus at night.
Jesus is loyal.	Judas betrayed Jesus at night.
Jesus can't be stopped.	Caiaphas's courtyard had a charcoal fire.
Jesus restores us.	Peter both denied Jesus and was restored by Jesus next to a charcoal fire.
Jesus transforms us.	Paul was blinded by a bright light.

Each **Storyline Bible Study** is five lessons long and can be paired with its thematic partner for a seamless ten-week study. Complement the *Saints* study with

SINNERS
EXPERIENCING JESUS' COMPASSION IN THE
MIDDLE OF YOUR SIN, STRUGGLES, AND SHAME

The *Sinners* Bible study will guide you through five stories of people considered sinful who acted with greater faith than the most religious people of Jesus' day.

LESSON ONE: Leaving Your Security Behind to Follow Jesus
> *The Tax Collector: The Faith of the Disciple Who Leaves*
> *His Tollbooth*
> MATTHEW 9

LESSON TWO: Advocating for Your Loved Ones with All You've Got
> *The Roman Centurion: The Faith of the Officer Who Advocates*
> *for His Sick Servant*
> LUKE 7

LESSON THREE: Offering Your Best to God Even When It Causes
a Commotion
> *The Sinful Woman: The Faith of the Outcast Who Anoints Jesus*
> LUKE 7

LESSON FOUR: Petitioning Jesus for Your Deepest Needs
> *The Canaanite Mom: The Faith of the Mother Who Begs Jesus*
> *to Heal Her Possessed Daughter*
> MATTHEW 15

LESSON FIVE: Announcing Jesus as Your Savior and the Savior
of the World
> *The Samaritan Woman: The Faith of the Woman at the Well*
> JOHN 4

Learn more at thestorylineproject.com.

CP1905

Storyline Bible Studies

Each study follows people, places, or things throughout the Bible.
This approach allows you to see the cohesive storyline of Scripture
and appreciate the Bible as the literary masterpiece that it is.

**Access free resources to help you teach or
lead a small group at thestorylineproject.com.**

STORYLINE

CP1816

Acknowledgments

WITHOUT MY FAMILY'S SUPPORT, the **Storyline Bible Studies** would just be a dream. I'm exceedingly grateful for a family that prays and cheers for me when I step out to try something new. To my husband, Aaron, son, Caleb, and mom, Noemi: You three sacrificed the most to ensure that I had enough time and space to write. Thank you. And to all my extended family: I know an army of Armstrongs was praying and my family in Austin was cheering me on to the finish line. Thank you.

To my ministry partners at the Polished Network, Integrus Leadership, and Dallas Bible Church: Linking arms with you made this project possible. I love doing Kingdom work with you.

NavPress and Tyndale teams: Thank you for believing in me. You wholeheartedly embraced the concept, and you've made this project better in every way possible. Special thanks to David Zimmerman, my amazing editor Caitlyn Carlson, Elizabeth Schroll, Olivia Eldredge, David Geeslin, and the entire editorial and marketing teams.

Jana Burson: You were the catalyst. Thank you.

Teresa Swanstrom Anderson: Thank you for connecting me with Caitlyn. You'll forever go down in history as the person who made my dreams come true.

All my friends rallied to pray for this project when I was stressed about the deadlines. Thank you. We did it! Without your intercession, these wouldn't be complete. I want to give special thanks to Ashton, Lee, Sarah, Amy, Tiffany, and Jenn for holding up my arms to complete the studies.

Resources for Deeper Study

OLD TESTAMENT
Bearing God's Name: Why Sinai Still Matters by Carmen Joy Imes

The Epic of Eden: A Christian Entry into the Old Testament by Sandra L. Richter

NEW TESTAMENT
Echoes of Scripture in the Gospels by Richard B. Hays

The Gospels as Stories: A Narrative Approach to Matthew, Mark, Luke, and John by Jeannine K. Brown

BIBLE STUDY
Commentary on the New Testament Use of the Old Testament, eds. G. K. Beale and D. A. Carson

Dictionary of Biblical Imagery, eds. Leland Ryken, James C. Wilhoit, and Tremper Longman III

The Drama of Scripture: Finding Our Place in the Biblical Story by Craig G. Bartholomew and Michael W. Goheen

From Beginning to Forever: A Study of the Grand Narrative of Scripture by Elizabeth Woodson

How (Not) to Read the Bible: Making Sense of the Anti-Women, Anti-Science, Pro-Violence, Pro-Slavery and Other Crazy Sounding Parts of Scripture by Dan Kimball

How to Read the Bible as Literature . . . and Get More Out of It by Leland Ryken

Literarily: How Understanding Bible Genres Transforms Bible Study by Kristie Anyabwile

The Mission of God: Unlocking the Bible's Grand Narrative by Christopher J. H. Wright

"Reading Scripture as a Coherent Story" by Richard Bauckham, in *The Art of Reading Scripture*, eds. Ellen F. Davis and Richard B. Hays

Reading While Black: African American Biblical Interpretation as an Exercise in Hope by Esau McCaulley

Read the Bible for a Change: Understanding and Responding to God's Word by Ray Lubeck

Scripture as Communication: Introducing Biblical Hermeneutics by Jeannine K. Brown

What Is the Bible and How Do We Understand It? by Dennis R. Edwards

Words of Delight: A Literary Introduction to the Bible by Leland Ryken

About the Author

KAT ARMSTRONG was born in Houston, Texas, where the humidity ruins her Mexi-German curls. She is a powerful voice in our generation as a sought-after Bible teacher. She holds a master's degree from Dallas Theological Seminary and is the author of *No More Holding Back*, *The In-Between Place*, and the **Storyline Bible Studies**. In 2008, Kat cofounded the Polished Network to embolden working women in their faith and work. Kat is pursuing a doctorate of ministry in New Testament context at Northern Seminary and is a board member of the Polished Network. She and her husband, Aaron, have been married for twenty years; live in Dallas, Texas, with their son, Caleb; and attend Dallas Bible Church, where Aaron serves as the lead pastor.

KATARMSTRONG.COM   THESTORYLINEPROJECT.COM
@KATARMSTRONG1   @THESTORYLINEPROJECT

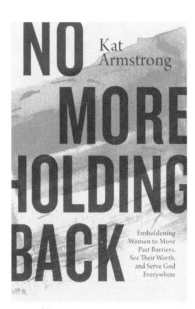

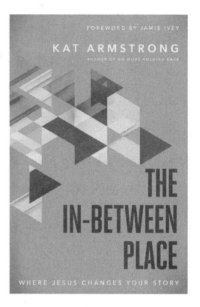

Make peace with your past.
Find hope in the present.
Step into your future.

CP1818

Notes

LESSON ONE | ACCEPTING JESUS' WORDS WHEN THEY CHALLENGE YOUR WORLDVIEW
1. Joseph Sievers and Amy-Jill Levine, eds., *The Pharisees* (Grand Rapids, MI: Eerdmans, 2021), ix.
2. Sievers and Levine, *The Pharisees*, xii.
3. Sievers and Levine, *The Pharisees*, xii.
4. Marianne Meye Thompson, *John: A Commentary*, The New Testament Library (Louisville, KY: Westminster John Knox Press, 2015), 78.
5. Pratap C. Gine and Jacob Cherian, "John," in *South Asia Bible Commentary: A One-Volume Commentary on the Whole Bible*, ed. Brian Wintle (Grand Rapids, MI: Zondervan, 2015), 1444.
6. Gine and Cherian, "John," in *South Asia Bible Commentary*, 1395.

LESSON TWO | REMAINING LOYAL TO JESUS WHEN YOU ARE TEMPTED TO BETRAY HIM
1. Apple Newsroom, "Apple's Global Phenomenon 'Ted Lasso' Joins Ranks of the Most Celebrated Comedies in History with Back-to-Back Emmy Wins for Outstanding Comedy Series at the 74th Primetime Emmy Awards," September 13, 2022, https://www.apple.com/newsroom/2022/09/apples-ted-lasso-wins-back-to-back-emmy-awards-for-outstanding-comedy-series.
2. Marianne Meye Thompson, *John: A Commentary*, The New Testament Library (Louisville, KY: Westminster John Knox Press, 2015), 163.
3. "Judas," from the *Holman Bible Dictionary*, accessed December 13, 2022, https://www.studylight.org/dictionaries/eng/hbd/j/judas.html.
4. Edward Sri, "Why Twelve?: The Apostles and the New Israel," St. Paul Center for Biblical Theology, November 18, 2019, https://stpaulcenter.com/why-twelve-the-apostles-and-the-new-israel.
5. Thompson, *John*, 261.

6. Mel Watkins, "Flip Wilson, Outrageous Comic and TV Host, Dies at 64," *New York Times*, November 27, 1998, https://www.nytimes.com/1998/11/27/arts/flip-wilson-outrageous-comic-and-tv-host-dies-at-64.html.

7. For an example of one of Wilson's "the devil made me do it" sketches, see https://www.youtube.com/watch?v=p88LY_IQBh0.

8. Thompson, *John*, 363.

LESSON THREE | USING YOUR INFLUENCE FOR GOOD WHEN IT DOESN'T BENEFIT YOU

1. James C. VanderKam, "High Priests," in *The Eerdmans Dictionary of Early Judaism*, John J. Collins and Daniel C. Harlow, eds. (Grand Rapids, MI: Eerdmans, 2010), 740–41.

2. Pratap C. Gine and Jacob Cherian, "John," in *South Asia Bible Commentary: A One-Volume Commentary on the Whole Bible*, ed. Brian Wintle (Grand Rapids, MI: Zondervan, 2015), 1423.

3. Gine and Cherian, "John," in *South Asia Bible Commentary*, 1423.

4. Marianne Meye Thompson, *John: A Commentary*, The New Testament Library (Louisville, KY: Westminster John Knox Press, 2015), 254.

LESSON FOUR | IDENTIFYING WITH JESUS WHEN YOUR REPUTATION IS ON THE LINE

1. For information on honor-shame cultures and how understanding them affects our understanding of the Gospels, see https://bibleproject.com/podcast/honor-shame-culture-and-gospel.

2. Pratap C. Gine and Jacob Cherian, "John," in *South Asia Bible Commentary: A One-Volume Commentary on the Whole Bible*, ed. Brian Wintle (Grand Rapids, MI: Zondervan, 2015), 1440.

3. Marianne Meye Thompson, *John: A Commentary*, The New Testament Library (Louisville, KY: Westminster John Knox Press, 2015), 440.

4. Eugene H. Peterson, *As Kingfishers Catch Fire: A Conversation on the Ways of God Formed by the Words of God* (Colorado Springs: WaterBrook, 2017), 357.

LESSON FIVE | REGAINING CLARITY WHEN YOU'RE BLINDED BY PASSION

1. Roland Deines, "Pharisees," in *The Eerdmans Dictionary of Early Judaism*, John J. Collins and Daniel C. Harlow, eds. (Grand Rapids, MI: Eerdmans, 2010), 1062.

2. Deines, "Pharisees," in *The Eerdmans Dictionary of Early Judaism*, 1062–63.

3. N. T. Wright and Michael F. Bird, *The New Testament in Its World: An Introduction to the History, Literature, and Theology of the First Christians* (Grand Rapids, MI: Zondervan Academic, 2019), 345.

4. Wright and Bird, *The New Testament in Its World*, 344.

5. Margaret Aymer, "Acts of the Apostles," in *Women's Bible Commentary*, 20th anniv. ed., Carol A. Newsom, Sharon H. Ringe, and Jacqueline E. Lapsley, eds. (Louisville, KY: Westminster John Knox Press, 2012), 541.

6. I. Howard Marshall, "Acts," in *Commentary on the New Testament Use of the Old Testament*, eds. G. K. Beale and D. A. Carson (Grand Rapids, MI: Baker Academic, 2007), 576.

7. Wright and Bird, *The New Testament in Its World*, 345.